Understanding Media:
A Popular Philosophy

Understanding Media:
A Popular Philosophy

Dominic Boyer

PRICKLY PARADIGM PRESS
CHICAGO

© 2007 Dominic Boyer
All rights reserved.

Prickly Paradigm Press, LLC
5629 South University Avenue
Chicago, Il 60637

www.prickly-paradigm.com

ISBN: 0-97940570-X
ISBN-13: 978-0-9794057-0-9
LCCN: 2007934315

Printed in the United States of America on acid-free paper.

If you're like me, you want to understand media because media seem so much the medium of contemporary life. Cell phones, email, the internet, instant messages, cable and satellite television, digital radio, webcams, PDAs, hotspots, podcasts, all these fabulous tools of communication and information that, within the past two decades or so, have passed from fantastic novelties into routine companions.

When we begin to think and talk about what distinguishes our contemporary moment, what gives us our historical and cultural identity, media are almost always on the table. Even correcting for the fact that not all—and not even close to most—human lives are as upper-middle-class, professional, well-traveled, and media-privileged as our own, it's hard to let go of the idea that media, especially new media, define today's world. Indeed, talking and thinking about media quickly comes to reference virtually everything else under the sun: the rhythms, the habits, the events, the values of contemporary life. How many times have you heard some variation on the wisdom that our lives are mediated, more so now than ever before? Under these circumstances, "understanding media" is no casual pursuit, not a choice but a necessity. And, to make things even more complicated, media change with such unsettling speed that it's hard even to keep track of what it is we need to understand. It's no secret among us media scholars at least that most of us are holding on for dear life, doing our best not to know less than we did the day before.

So we write and we talk, constantly, about media, contributing each in our own ways to the overall impression that media are the center of contemporary human experience. There are texts—ranging from academic books to magazine articles to blogs and wikis—that will help you to understand in great detail and with technical precision how, for example, internet search engines work, or, how the 1996 U.S. Telecommunications Act reshaped American broadcasting, or, what "next generation" telephony will look like, or, how digital information technologies might transform mundane objects like clothing and home appliances over the next few decades.

Given the dizzying spectacle of media knowledge already out there, why a "popular philosophy"? For the very reason of the abundance of what is already out there. Think of this as a guidebook that offers some orientation in the wilderness of media talk and media thinking today. But unlike GPS, Mapquest, or, in case anyone recalls, Baedeker's, this isn't the kind of navigational instrument that is going to lead you into the back alleys of distant places. Nor is it equipped to explain to you exactly what you will find there. The pages of this text explain and explore our common habits of thinking about media rather than offering another geography or inventory of our media worlds.

Why pay attention to our common habits of media talk and thinking? It has struck me in working in and around media studies for the past decade that as much as we need to know, specifically, where we are (and where we are going) in our contemporary ecology of media, we need a more basic kind of orientation as well. We need to know better why we understand media and our relationship to media in the terms that we do. Those questions all too often get lost in the rush of details, not because the questions are trivial but because they involve assumptions that we almost have to make in order to create and communicate knowledge about details.

These assumptions—our taken for granted ways of thinking about media—are the main topic of this essay. To give a few examples that I return to at greater length below: why is it that so many of us feel so comfortable talking about "the media" as though it were a singular entity even when we also know the great complexity and diversity of contemporary modes of mass communication? Why do we assume that new media technologies like the internet have the capacity to transform, perhaps even radically transform, human culture? Why is it that we often treat "mediation" as one of the central, perhaps even as the central, feature of modern human experience but that we also struggle so hard to find adequate terms with which to discuss it? How can we routinely describe media as tools, as instruments for fulfilling human purposes like communication, yet also speak of them just as routinely as excessive, powerful, and invasive forces that we have no hope of taming?

• • • •

These questions, and others like them, are the medium of the pages that follow. Above all, I seek to show how our perceptions and certainties about media are shaped by our desire to define ourselves as active agents in a world that often seems saturated with social mediation—I'll explain what I mean by that later on. For the moment, let's just say that the scale and complexity of media and mediation challenge our ability to understand them with the same certainty, for example, that we understand ourselves and our more immediate actions and environs. So, the problem of certainty is another major theme of this essay, as is how anxieties and fantasies are always braided into our certainties about media.

Please take seriously my use of the plural, "certainties." My use of "we" in this text is not meant to indicate that I believe that all of "us" think about media in the same ways. Far from it. But I do argue here that there are some attentions and habits in understanding media that are so widespread that it is impossible to explain them as a matter of individual opinions or judgments. Indeed, they are social judgments—

speaking to the fact that human social relations and institutions broker the encounter of self and world—and they thus require social explanations.

This brings me to a last point concerning this popular philosophy as guidebook. Most guidebooks offer tours of the unknown, or at least of the not sufficiently known. I could scarcely make this claim about media. We are all, all of us, in our own ways, expert media makers and users and occasional media philosophers. But we all also make and use media differently and inhabit differently composed media environments. And so, by extension, we know different media and we engage them with different levels of intimacy and comfort. Taking nothing away from the richness and importance of personal experiences of media, the purpose of media studies as a discipline is coordinative, bringing elements of our various media experiences and knowledges together into alignment with one another. If nothing else, even if it tells you what you already know, the synthetic work of media studies has legitimational value in that it can validate personal experience comparatively and an expansionary value in that when it invalidates personal experience it can offer alternative ways in which to understand. So mine is a popular philosophy that fully expects that what it has to say will be both familiar and strange—how could a discussion of our habits of thinking about media be anything else? My experience teaching about media has taught me that this is a good approach. Even the most expert media makers and knowers among us remain tremendously curious about how else they might understand media. Because media is such an intrinsically broad, complex and dynamic subject, one is never surprised at being surprised by something unexpected.

The title of this essay offers one such twist. I began this essay in 2004 on the fortieth anniversary of the publication of Marshall McLuhan's book, *Understanding Media*, and approached it as a rethinking of that book's project in the context of media today. Although, as you will gather soon enough, I have reservations about McLuhan's media theory, I think one must fairly acknowledge that *Understanding Media* was revolutionary as few books are for reshaping both expert and commonsense understandings of their subject matter for years to come. Sigmund Freud's *The Interpretation of Dreams* was another such book—and, where Freud gave us a new set of tools for decoding the messages of dreams in relation to the structures of the psyche, McLuhan gave us the idea of the medium as "message," that media were nothing less than the central complex of forces shaping human history and human culture. McLuhan's core argument was that everything else we might think influenced media (let's say human ideas, intentions, or values) could be shown instead to be functions of particular media environments. Heady stuff for 1964—it's no wonder that McLuhan became the pop culture guru that he did even though today his book seems almost tame compared to what one might find prophesied in the pages of magazines like *Wired*. More than coining memorable catchphrases like "the global village" and "the medium is the message," McLuhan found the words to voice a new sensibility concerning media and mediation that had accumulated over the course of the 19th and 20th centuries. I explain below what I find insightful and blind about this sensibility but, for the moment, put simply, my twist on McLuhan's title is one of emphasis. McLuhan's book was about media, about "Understanding *Media*," and it offered a wild ride, unapologetically diverting itself from familiar media territory like newspapers, radio and television into unexpected excurses on clocks, clothing, money, cars and government. Although I hope my project stays true to McLuhan's spirit of iconoclasm, it has different ambitions—this text is less about theorizing our new media ecology per se then about media understanding, about "*Understanding* Media." I want to ask how it is possible for us to think about media in the ways that we commonly do. In this essay, I seek to tell a more complex story of our experience and understanding of "being mediated," including, not least, how someone like McLuhan was able to recognize the "message" of media in the way that he did.

I

Talking Media, Thinking Media

Since, as already noted, this text contributes to a vast expanse of knowledge about media, the first section of the essay engages past and present thinking about media in order to answer the question: Where does all this media talk come from? And, where better to begin talking about media talk then with:

"The media"

Now, there's nothing that rolls off the tongue quite like "the media." We hear a lot about it (or them) these days and what they are up to, and also about liberal media, conservative media, religious media, corporate media, alternative media, new media, old media, and on and on. Sometimes the media are praised, but more often probably criticized or indicted for something they did or failed to do. To confirm this suspicion, I used a remarkable media instrument, Google.com, to search instances of the phrase "the problem with the media..." on the internet. I received 13,500 hits. Meanwhile, variations on the phrase, "the good thing about the media..." received no more than 45 hits.

Value judgments aside, in all cases, "the media" seem to be there, everywhere, equally as danger and opportunity, pervading social experience, recasting relations of privacy and publicity, channeling and amplifying communication, shifting the speed of inter-action, creating new possibilities of expression and reception even as they threaten new powers of surveil-lance and documentation. Talk about "the media" cuts across political sympathies, across generations, across professions and social strata—in a culture that prides itself on diversity, "the media" is a remarkably uniform and unremarkable category, even in satire. My favorite line from *Da Ali G Show* comes in an interview with C. Everett Koop where Ali asks, "Does all of us really have bones or is that just what the media wants us to believe?" It's a hilarious moment because the joke is already on us—television interviews are overflowing with claims about the influence "the media" exercises over our perception of the world. Koop, anyway, scarcely flinches.

The ubiquity of talk about the media is a curi-ous social fact only when one considers that this use of the word, "media"—as singular noun and collective subject to condense and describe institutions and instruments of mass communication—is of rather recent origin. According to the *Oxford English*

Dictionary, this use of the word, "media," only developed in the 1920s and then within the relatively narrow confines of the advertising industry. Until the mid 19th century, "media" had no greater significance than as the plural form of the word "medium," derived from the Latin *medius*, or "middle." Gradually, after the mid 19th century "media" developed its first technical meaning of its own (that is, not simply as a pluralized form of "medium"), a medical reference to the middle membrane of an artery or vessel. Later, "media" was recoined in professional advertising discourse to describe the vehicles of advertisements—for example, newspapers and magazines (even generating a curious new plural form, "medias")—and thereby developed the kernel of its present set of associations. Rather quickly, given the publicity inherent to advertising, it began to spread into other communities of media experts and entered public culture with full force in the 1950s and 1960s. Still, "the media" only attained widespread popular usage in the 1970s and 1980s. And, yet, today, only a generation later, it's difficult to think about media in any other way except as a powerful, collective subject.

So how did we get here? First of all, long before ubiquitous talk about "the media" we had ubiquitous talk about "the press," which was a popular feature of European and American political culture dating well back into the 18th century. "The press" referred most often to political editorialism, especially to journalists and publications critical of the reigning authorities—"the press" was typically reviled or celebrated for the liberties it sought to take in its efforts to promote truth (according to its supporters) or deception (according to its detractors). "The media" is still often used in this sense in the forums of contemporary political culture, from congressional debate to cable news shoutfests, but it also clearly maintains a diversity of meanings beyond this.

The story of "media" becomes more interesting when one also looks into the linguistic history of its original singular form, "medium," more closely. "Medium" has had a rather rich and varied history of usage in English since the beginning of the 17th century, having been employed in many ways to express middle qualities, conditions, or states of in-betweenness. Sometimes the uses have been more sober and scientific, for example, as a synonym for an arithmetical mean or average. But, more often, it seems "medium" was employed with a certain poetic license, to capture any intervening substance or environment that carried a force from place to another, or, as Joseph Worcester's 1860 dictionary had it, "That through which a body, not in contact with another, must pass to reach it; space or substance passed through; any thing intervening." Thus, also the mesmerist notion of the "medium" as subject of animal magnetism or the spiritualist notion of the "medium" as a means of communication with departed spirits.

More to the point, connected to this principal definition of "any thing intervening" was a secondary definition of "medium" that has become more primary for "media" in the 20th century: the "instrumentality" or "means" through which something else was transferred or achieved. Worcester offers the example of money, "Money is the medium of exchanges." As its earliest recorded use, the *OED* offers Francis Bacon's apt observation, "But yet is not of necessitie that Cogitations bee expressed by the Medium of Wordes" (1605).

So, there are two core meanings to "medium" which today's "media" has also inherited: that which lies between and that which serves as the instrument of something else—the middle ground and the means.

And, yet, as illuminating as this etymological history might be, it also does not quite explain the sense of totality and ubiquity that often accompanies uses of the term "media" or "the media" today. We hear constantly that we are awash in media of all different kinds and that these media may be radically reorganizing human experience. Under these circumstances, who doubts "the media" exist and that they are efficacious, in other words, that they exert some kind of integrated, even singular, influence in the world? Usage of the term is now so commonplace that it appears in all sorts of offhand everyday remarks like: "the media got ahold of that story;" "the media is blowing it all out of proportion;" and "what are the media saying about it?" And, of course, we note that people working in "the media" never tire of talking about "the media," which actually seems somehow to assure the reality of the whole enterprise. But what are they actually talking about? No one really bothers to define "the media," perhaps because they're "the media," they don't need defining (almost by definition).

Noting the ubiquity only raises other questions: such as, why? Why is talk of the media so intuitive and pervasive today? When some seemingly new force emerges in human history, and receives this kind of popular recognition, that force is worthy of serious scrutiny, because, in all honesty, new forces don't emerge in human history all that often. But I must admit that, even as a media scholar—that is, as someone whose livelihood is wrapped up in media existing—I often find both scholarly and popular discussions of media mysterious. "The media" has become one of those terms like "the government" or "the market" that are used to talk about forces that are extensive, abstract and complex, unknowable in the details of their supposed entireties, but, at the same time, immediate, pervasive, and banal in important ways. We all believe these entities exist but all of us, even the experts, would be hard pressed to reach a collective consensus as to what they are, let alone what they mean for us.

To put this another way, phrases like "the media" serve as linguistic glosses, the kinds of routine placeholders in language that allow communication and knowledge to move forward where gaps emerge in our experiential knowledge of the forces at work in the world "out there." Because we all have our precise attentions (or expertise) about matters great and small that we have developed throughout our lives, but never about everything in human experience. And, when we exceed our zones of more precise attention in conversation, as we inevitably have to do, we often shade in the grey areas with placeholders. I like to think of them like the bridges over space that frequently crop up in adventure movies accompanied by the advice, "Whatever you do, don't look down!"

What lies beneath, in this case, is our absent or uncertain experiential knowledge and yet, again, simply because it is impossible to know everything, it is inevitable and ordinary that we span such gaps. Linguistic glosses come in handy in communication when we sense that none of the partners to the situation really want or plan to look down into the chasms below. And this is perhaps why no one—not even the media experts—ever really bothers to define "the media" anymore. On the one hand, it simply wouldn't be worth the trouble to define further this sense of the immense social power and pressure of mass communication that many of us share. On the other hand, a serious pause to acknowledge the complexity and pervasiveness of mass communication is enough to make anyone panicky. How could we possibly begin to understand the totality that "the media" pretends to capture? So, we opt for the safer route as we start out over the bridge. Better not to look down.

Yet, failing to acknowledge that decision is where mischief arises. Because it is then all too possible to behave as though our glosses really do represent the truth of the world "out there" rather than the result of necessary efforts to simplify and domesticate it. In turn, the frequency, ubiquity and aptness of the placeholders become powerful influences upon how we know the world around us, they become vastly important conceptual and experiential categories, the stakes from which we pitch our tents of knowledge. To take a different example, categories of national identity are particularly efficacious in this way. If you have read the op-ed page of an American newspaper recently you know that they are filled with such talk—the meaning of "being American" or the content of "American values" elicit endless conversation but rarely consensus without recourse to yet another gloss like "freedom" or "liberty." So, Americans love freedom, who could really disagree? But, freedom for whom and to do what? And, how is loving freedom somehow an distinctively American quality? Where, for example, would we find the bondage loving peoples to whom we are contrasting ourselves? My friend and fellow media scholar, Francis Nyamnjoh, once put it rather well, "Show me any human being who does not prize his or her freedom!" The "debates" over American values, if they can be so called, circle around and around the same territory and positions and yet, all the same, they seem to elicit ever-renewed enthusiasm from their participants since no one of them seems to doubt that "being American" is something meaning-ful and worth arguing over. That is the point. Even if there is little agreement on the substance of American-ness and on who or what best exemplifies its virtues, we find consensus and certainty in the existence of the category itself—such categories are, if you will, the medium of our culture. Just so, in our present circum-stances, "the media." And this is why seeking to understand media both presents us with a challenging impasse and entices us with the promise of a way to puzzle through contemporary human social experi-ence more broadly.

Understanding media
(in the medium of McLuhan)

Understanding "the media" brings us back to Marshall McLuhan and his message of the centrality of media to all human experience. After suffering a slow descent into obscurity in the 1970s, the past ten years or so have witnessed the makings of a McLuhan renaissance. There has been an academic side of this renaissance where some in media studies have embraced McLuhan as a prescient media analyst with ideas years ahead of his time. And, even when he is criticized for his methods and hyperbole, it is clear that McLuhan is, once again, relevant. But, above all, McLuhan has found new life in the public culture that mushroomed around new media and information technologies in the 1980s and 1990s, in magazines like *Wired*, for example, which embraced him as something of a patron saint for the digital revolution.

Finding the right label for McLuhan isn't my task here. My concern is with how and why McLuhan understood media in the terms that he did. On the face of it, McLuhan's relationship to media seems a study in contradictions, if not paradoxes. Despite a solid if unremarkable career as a literary scholar trained by two giants of New Criticism, I.A. Richards and F.R. Leavis, at Cambridge, and despite a life-long love of bookish erudition sustained within the relative comforts of an academic position at the University of Toronto, it seems curious that McLuhan spent much of his later life expressing disdain for the kind of literate mindset that continually overestimated the power of books and reading to transform the world. It's not that McLuhan thought books were irrelevant to human history, far from it; rather, he felt that the machinery of the printing press had already transformed the world and radically so, producing, among other things, the nationalism, individualism, and visual orientation of modern Western culture. But the culture of the printing press that had come into its own in the 16th and 17th centuries was waning, McLuhan argued, and we of the literate West repressed acknowledgment of the coming culture of digital or "electronic media" (as he termed them) at our own peril. McLuhan's *Understanding Media* was meant to be a first book of the digital era, a book whose forays into the social effects and forms wrought by electronic communication would shake the dying tree of print culture to its roots. McLuhan's academic mentor Richards once warned of the "sinister potentialities of the cinema and the loudspeaker" to decay Western civilization as he knew it. McLuhan would come to agree, but also to embrace the state of transformation; with *Understanding Media*, Richards' student sought to refunction the book from a typographic "ditto device" into an amplifier.

Looking back, McLuhan's amplified voice—a steady, authoritative baritone—was heard in the 1960s. Even if his messages did not always transmit clearly, they echoed widely. In the end, McLuhan's resonance, and his desired resonance, became stronger outside academic culture, among artists from Woody Allen to Andy Warhol, among the literary avant-garde of the diverse likes of Wyndham Lewis, Norman Mailer and George Steiner, and among a growing business intelligentsia spread across corporate "creative" fields like marketing, design, advertising and so on. McLuhan's work seemed particularly seductive and legitimating for a young generation of corporate futurists who were busy mounting their own revolution against the Taylorist and Fordist organization of industrial production, thus inaugurating the regime of perpetual innovation and flexible production under which we currently live. In an essay for the *New York Herald Tribune*, Tom Wolfe went so far as to describe McLuhan as the Delphic oracle of the corporate world A.D. 1965. To give you a sense of the Zeitgeist here is how Wolfe's essay begins:

WHAT IF HE IS RIGHT? There are currently hundreds of studs of the business world, breakfast food package designers, television network creative department vice-presidents, advertising "media-reps", lighting fixture fortune heirs, smiley patent lawyers, industrial spies, we-need-vision board chairmen, all sorts of business studs who are all wondering if this man, Marshall McLuhan … is right … Suppose he is what he sounds like, the most important thinker since Newton, Darwin, Freud, Einstein, and Pavlov, studs of the intelligentsia game—suppose he is the oracle of the modern times—*what if he is right*? …An "undisclosed corporation" has put a huge "undisclosed sum" into McLuhan's Centre for Culture and Technology at the University of Toronto. One of the big American corporations has offered him $5000 to present a closed-circuit—ours!—television lecture on—oracle!—the way the products in its industry will be used in the future. Even before this, IBM, General Electric, Bell Telephone were flying McLuhan in from Toronto to New York, Pittsburgh, God knows where else, to talk to their hierarchs about ... well, about whatever this unseen world of electronic environments that only he sees fully is all about.

If, as I noted above, the semantic road from "medium" to "the media" was already well into its paving by the time of McLuhan's appearance on the public scene in the late 1950s, McLuhan distinguished himself over the subsequent decade by offering a new way of reading human history and culture through the lens of media. Even if his story didn't persuade everyone, its very existence was pivotal in cementing media's status as a force to be reckoned with in human experience. Even to refute McLuhan was to accept his terms that media exerted a historical force at least equal to, if not greater than, other forces that had previously been placed at the center of the philosophy of history such as divine imagination or doctrine, human will or civilization, and natural ecologies or evolution.

McLuhan's innovation, for better or for worse, was to rewrite the philosophy of history in the medium of media. In the second paragraph of *Understanding Media*, he wrote:

> For the "message" of any medium or technology is the change of scale or pace or pattern that it introduces into human affairs. The railway did not introduce movement or transportation or wheel or road into human society, but it accelerated and enlarged the scale of previous human functions, creating totally new kinds of cities and new kinds of work and leisure. This happened whether the railway functioned in a tropical or a northern environment,

and is quite independent of the freight or content of the railway medium. The airplane, on the other hand, by accelerating the rate of transportation, tends to dissolve the railway form of city, politics, and association, quite independently of what the airplane is used for.

Absorbing ideas that had already emerged within the nascent field of cybernetics in the 1940s and 1950s, McLuhan understood media in essence as "extensions" of the human senses, faculties, and capacities. For example, the wheel, McLuhan wrote, is an extension of the mobile capacities of the foot and the book an extension of the visual capacities of the eye. But a wheel obviously has different intrinsic properties than a foot does. Media were prosthetic in the sense that they extended human power or "agency" in the world. But, McLuhan argued that these prosthetics also redefined, reproportioned and rescaled human powers in fundamental ways. Once reliant upon a prosthesis we could never walk or see or act the same way again. The real power, according to McLuhan, was in the prosthesis, not in the person. Thus, the entire fabric of human experience inevitably changed as our ecology of extensions evolved. And, McLuhan believed that human history had proceeded through distinct cultural stages in which different senses and their extensions predominated.

This process began with tribal culture, a "culture of the ear and mouth" as McLuhan put it, which found its social apex and epitome in the environment of the tribal fire ("an acoustic, horizonless, boundless, olfactory space rather than… visual space") around which human beings gathered to commune with each other, entranced by their multisensory apprehension of the world. This mythic, history-less existence was disrupted, according to McLuhan, only by the early civilizations whose new media extensions like papyrus or clay tablets reshuffled human senses and capacities of action. But it was early Western civilization that distanced itself most profoundly from tribal culture, McLuhan claimed, first by the invention of the phonetic alphabet and then, centuries later, by the further technical extension of typography. Both propelled vision to dominance among the human senses since he argued that alphabets and typography saturated human experience with abstract codes that necessitated constant visual engagement and decoding.[1] The rise of visual dominance in turn catalyzed broader cultural shifts according to McLuhan, radically curtailing the social significance of other senses like hearing and touch, and making "visualist" principles

---

[1]McLuhan Sidebar: The equation of literacy and visualism is one of McLuhan's most important and contestable claims. Historically, mass literacy in Europe was not achieved with the advent of typography but only through civic and religious education programs that accelerated in the latter half of the 19th century. Until this point, an argument about the cultural effects of literacy would have to be limited to the literate societal elite (less than 5% of the population in many parts of Europe). But, one could counter, McLuhan's argument is really more cognitivist than historicist. Here, other challenges can be raised against McLuhan's equation. Although reading indeed involves vision, neurological research suggests that much of the work of literacy occurs in the language processing centers of the brain rather than in the primary visual cortex or in the secondary visual processing areas (responsible for spatial awareness, among other things). A linguistic message conveyed by an auditory stimulus (like listening to radio) would actually be

like divisibility, instrumentality, objectivity, "uniformity, continuity, and lineality" into the institutions of modern Western culture. In a nutshell, literate Western Man came to engage the world as an abstract visual object and sought to dominate it and bend it to his purposes through his modern machineries of administration, science and war. At the same time, despite Western colonialism and imperialism, tribal culture never died out, but was forced instead to the margins of the predatory West, living on, McLuhan argued, in the cultures of modern non-Western peoples in Africa, Asia and Oceania.

True to his oracular vocation, it was a third, emergent, stage of human culture that interested McLuhan even more than tribal or literate humanity. The visualist culture of the modern West was now being eroded from within, McLuhan argued, by the new social and sensory effects of electricity. Beginning with telephony and telegraphy in the 19th century and

---

handled largely in the same sequence (albeit by different pathways) in the language processing, symbol-coding and -decoding centers of the brain. Moreover, there is really no neurological evidence at this time to suggest that reading a lot predictably heightens one's visual disposition beyond reading. So, while one might still wish to argue that Western civilization is distinctively "visualist," one would have to look elsewhere than the interface of print media and the senses to explain it. The anthropological research of Faye Ginsburg, Eric Michaels and Terence Turner, among others, has also shown that modern non-Western cultures maintain highly sophisticated practices of visual representation even in the absence of alphabetic literacy. For anthropologists, McLuhan's narrative of the fall of multisensory tribal culture into monosensory modern culture is suspect for its echoes of Enlightenment myths of "the noble savage" and his fall from grace. In short, the "culture of the ear and mouth" is largely a fallacy.

accelerated by the mass expansion of radio and television in the 20th century, McLuhan noted how electric communication had come to saturate the social experience of the modern West. Electricity was, for McLuhan, pure speed and pure information. Its speed portended an unprecedented condensation of time and space for humanity while its capacity for information transfer free of a material shell augured an unprecedented tension between what latter day McLuhanite media guru Nicholas Negroponte would call the worlds of "bits and atoms." On both counts, McLuhan controversially predicted enormous cultural shifts, the tip of whose iceberg he outlined in *Understanding Media*.

McLuhan was unsurprised that the institutions and impresarios of literate culture were resistant to his message of a dawning electric culture. McLuhan warned that we Western men and women, as creatures of a hot sensorium of literacy, were poorly equipped to recognize and to appreciate the cool sensorium of electric media. McLuhan meant "hot" in the informatic sense of high definition, of media that cultivated one of the human senses intensively by providing it with an abundance of data. "Cool" media by contrast were low definition and tended to be multisensory—like television, or better yet, the internet, which McLuhan would have recognized as a paradigmatic instance of electric culture both for its capacity of instantaneous information transfers and for its participatory and multisensory character. Electric culture meant new modes of human intimacy and contact, it meant a reawakening of suppressed senses like tactility and hearing, it meant new powers of information coupled to a loss of centralized control over the world. Here McLuhan sketched what French philosophers Gilles Deleuze and Felix Guattari would later call the "rhizomatic" character of the contemporary. Electric culture was not only something qualitatively new, it was also restorative, reactivating cultural tendencies from the earliest phase of human history, renewing tribalism, the culture of the ear and mouth. But this was no easy process according to him a true revolution never is: "We are no more prepared to encounter radio and TV in our literate milieu than the native of Ghana is able to cope with the literacy that takes him out of his collective tribal world and beaches him in individual isolation," McLuhan wrote, "We are as numb in our new electric world as the native involved in our literate and mechanical culture."

McLuhan's principle metaphor for our emergent cultural state was "the global village," a state of informational interdependency and immediacy created by electricity. McLuhan liked to liken the instantaneity and ubiquity of electronic news reports, for example, to the echoing of a mythic tribal drum throughout the African jungle. Four years before the publication of *Understanding Media*, in a television interview with Alan Millar for the Canadian Broadcast Corporation in 1960, McLuhan explained:

> MM: These new media have made our world into a single unit. The world now is like a continuously sounding tribal drum where everybody gets the message all the time. A princess gets married in England and boom, boom, boom, sound the drums. We all hear about it. An earthquake in North

Africa, a Hollywood star gets drunk. Away go the drums again...

AM: Why, Marshall, do you use the word "tribal"?

MM: Well, I think you'll find everything we've observed tonight about the media points in the direction of tribal man and away from individual man.

AM: By individual man I assume you are referring to literary man?

MM: Yes and tribal man is the man created by the new electronic media... Yes, we're retribalizing. Involuntarily we're getting rid of individualism. We're in a process of making a tribe. For just as books and their private point of view are being replaced by the new media, so the actions, the concepts that underlie our social life are changing. We're no longer so concerned with self-definition, with finding our own individual way. We're more concerned with what the group knows, with feeling as its does and acting with it.

Note that there is something quite compelling about the image of the global village today, even more so perhaps than in the 1960s. McLuhan seemed to relish the unsettling intimation that Western technological progress was beginning to devour itself. With electric culture, every new invention was also a civilizational step backward. The linear sense of time and the Cartesian coordinates of space that McLuhan associated with visual literacy and modern society were doomed by the proliferation of electric media and the disruptive excessive speed and reach of their information flows. So, Western civilization was fated to decline by its own most modern technologies, technologies that were universal extensions of humanity in ways that could no longer be managed or dominated by any one part of it.

At least, so McLuhan's assumed—there was no talk yet of a "digital divide" in the 1960s and McLuhan did not live to see how the end of Cold War geopolitics and subsequent "new world orders" failed to emancipate the world from the existence of centers of economic, political and military domination. But his image of the global village has survived, displaying impressive symbolic tenacity. Even in the face of evidence of enduring social inequities surrounding (and in many cases reinforced by) new media technologies, there is ceaseless media talk these days about the universal and emancipatory potentials of new media. Some thirty years after *Understanding Media*, Negroponte predicted again that digital media would soon initiate social and political revolutions from within, extending outward across the world, "Digital technology can be a natural force drawing people into greater world harmony.... The access, the mobility, and the ability to effect change are what will make the future so different from the present." New media talk almost always predicts a universal harmonizing effect— as though the very fact of an internet were proof alone of a coming global unity. And, yet, as media theorist Geert Lovink has pointed out, the vast majority of digital mediation remains highly localized and limited in both its reach and its outlook on the world. This seems to be increasingly the case as the internet expands and vernacularizes. For example, the internet is increasingly multilingual with English usage dipping recently under 30% for the first time. As far as digital mediation goes, the world is far removed from a harmonized cultural unit and new media offer as many opportunities for cultural diversification as for "retribalization."

In defense of McLuhan, he never said that the global village promised a perfect future. Consider two passages from *Understanding Media*, one from near the beginning and the other from the end, that illustrate his effort to think through the implications of the global village for humanity.

> Electromagnetic technology requires utter human docility and quiescence of meditation such as befits an organism that now wears its brain outside its skull and its nerves outside its hide. Man must serve his electric technology with the same servo-mechanistic fidelity with which he served his coracle, his canoe, his typography, and all other extensions of his physical organs. But there is a difference, that previous technologies were partial and fragmentary, and the electric is total and inclusive. An external consensus or conscience is now as necessary as private consciousness. With the new media, however, it is also possible to store and to translate everything; and, as for speed, that is no problem. No further acceleration is possible this side of the light barrier.

> But with electricity and automation, the technology of fragmented processes suddenly fused with the human dialogue and the need for over-all consideration of human unity. Men are suddenly nomadic

> gatherers of knowledge, nomadic as never before, informed as never before, free from fragmentary specialism as never before—but also involved in the total social process as never before; since, with electricity we extend our central nervous system globally, instantly interrelating every human experience.

There is a restlessness within McLuhan's vision of electric culture. It is not clear whether he thinks electric culture is good or bad and he likely would have preferred to say that is simply was. Nevertheless the language of fidelity and servitude does not suggest that electric culture offers any kind of redemption for humanity through technology. Electric media may free us from the forms of social power distinctive of visualist literate culture but they also reconfigure the scale and speed of social power, making "external consensus" and social involvement as important as private conscience once was. Yet this fidelity to media was in no way special to electric media, McLuhan commented—fidelity is what all media extensions demand.

And, cutting now to the chase, *this* is precisely "the message" of McLuhan's media theory. McLuhan's core argument was that human beings stand in a largely reactive state to their media extensions. We do not control these extensions as tools even though we may utilize them in tool-like ways. Instead, we must respect that media have the capacity to "work us over completely" as McLuhan was fond of saying. For all intents and purposes, they define our culture for us. What is distinctive about McLuhan's philosophy is that media begin to take on a curious life of their own. Indeed it might be more accurate to describe humanity as the medium of media rather than the other way around. And this is where we must break away from McLuhan's philosophy to pose a few more general and daunting questions: how is it possible to understand media in these terms? And why is that such an understanding of media seems even more plausible today than it did at the time that McLuhan was writing?

Beyond McLuhan: understanding the poetic, the formal and the medial

I've dwelled so long on McLuhan not just because of the intrinsic interest of his work. My point is to elicit a resonance across time. I suspect and hope that you have been able to find something strangely familiar in McLuhan's understanding of media. I would argue that a good deal of contemporary thinking about media is latently, if not explicitly, McLuhanite in its orientation. By this I mean that McLuhan's cybernetic sense of the governance of media and mediation over human consciousness, action and society has become a more general sensibility in understanding media. There is something of McLuhan even in simple, everyday talk about "the media." Yet I am not claiming that McLuhan's way of understanding media became widespread because he truly was an oracle, or because he was such a genius that he saw things that no one else saw.

I actually mean to argue the opposite—McLuhan could write what he wrote because he expressed something that was already becoming a common intuition in the culture around him. Like a thunderhead that gathers beyond the horizon only to announce itself through a spectacular cloudburst. I would describe McLuhan's media theory not as a beginning but rather as a kind of culminating, gathering point for a rising sense, across the 19th and 20th centuries, of the presence and social importance of what I will term "the medial" dimension of human life. McLuhan was not the first scholar to recognize the significance of the medial (the evidence of Bacon's "Medium" or of Plato's comparison of the virtues of writing and oratory in his *Phaedrus* suggests that this is a very old recognition for philosophy). He was not even the first scholar to propose that the medial was "the message" of contemporary social life, capable of working us over completely—I explain below that that honor belongs to Karl Marx's theory of capital.

But McLuhan did distinguish himself by translating an apprehension of the rising significance of the medial into a theory of "media" and in writing a philosophy of history with media as its propellant force. As such, McLuhan both inherited a long philosophical tradition of thinking about mediation and effectively translated and streamlined this tradition into a contemporary idiom that resonated marvelously at a historical moment (the 1960s) when there was great popular fascination with, and concern about, the social and psychological effects of new mass communication and information technologies, especially television. Thus McLuhan became a gateway to the popularization of a sense of media as a collective force in human history, and, in important ways, to the crystallization of a language of "the media" as a collective force "out there" exercising powerful and perhaps decisive influence over our forms of contemporary life.

To explain what I mean by "the medial," I need to contrast it, really to place it between, two other terms: the poetic and the formal. I mean "poetic" here in the sense of its Greek roots of a principle of creation or "bringing forth" and "formal" in the Latin sense of stable shape. The poetic-medial-formal triad has represented a fairly constant arrangement in Western philosophy since the Greeks, although one can find partial analogies for it in many non-Western philosophies and cosmologies as well. At its core, the triad provides a very rough schematic of being, distinguishing between an internal, creative force extending itself into the world (the poetic), a state of formality, somehow external to the poetic, that can be viewed as a realization of the poetic, or, as in some Christian spirit/body dualities, antithetical to the poetic (the formal), and a third term, conveying that which stands in between the poetic and the formal, sometimes a residual or passive domain, sometimes a domain that is said to transform fundamentally the character of both the poetic and the formal (the medial).

Let me emphasize that how this triad is posited and how its elements are distinguished from one another is eminently flexible and varies from religion to religion, culture to culture, and philosophy to philosophy. Philosophically, the triad can be taken literally as ontological, a matter of being, or as phenomenological, a question of being in time and in the world, or as epistemological, a state of knowledge that we have about the world and ourselves. The poetic can be defined as the presence of a divine spirit, or of the human spirit, acting in accord with a divine mission or fate, or of a human spirit creating human life from materials at hand in the world, or of the realm of imagination and creativity contrasted to a realm of mechanical existence and the senses, and so on. The formal can refer to the human flesh, to the materiality of the world, to the artifacts produced by the poetic, to a realm of objects contrasted to a realm of subjects, and so on. And, the medial, perhaps the most vexing and elusive category of all, can refer to the instruments of poetic expression, to the middle-ground between creativity and habit, to the domain of human interconnection and sociality and its modes of exchange and reproduction (e.g., language, transaction, and so on). Always it refers to that which lies "in between" and thus connects very closely to the two meanings of "medium" we recovered above: the middle-ground and the means. In Western philosophy before the late 18th century the medial often has a relatively vestigial existence. The existence of middles, means, and media are always recognized but usually treated as unpowerful in themselves and thus of secondary philosophical significance to the poetic and the formal. Thus, in contemporary secular Western culture, it is not uncommon to merge the medial and the formal, as in discussions of the circulating power of commodities and technologies. But, in other Christian cultures, including contemporary ones, the medial and the poetic have been in stronger alignment via faith in the harmonious transfers between souls and an immanent, ever-circulating divine spirit. In many Melanesian societies, the poetic/medial distinction is likewise quite fluid, but in a different way, with persons able to share themselves with each other via exchange objects that can literally carry personality across space and time. To reiterate, cultural and historical variance is paramount in philosophy. And, yet, such philosophical distinctions and categories as what I am terming (in the abstract) the poetic, the medial and the formal, also cross and unite human societies and cultures simply because they refer to experiential conditions common to all of them.

So, the specific story I would like tell, a very abridged one I am afraid, is of the historical emergence of a category of "the medial" in Western philosophy and social science since the late 18th century that was no longer viewed as a residual category of human experience but rather as an increasingly central and powerful one. It is, of course, never the case that the medial supplants the poetic and the formal altogether as categories of intuition and knowledge even if, in some cases, like McLuhan's, it seems to come closer to doing so. This story is less about the dwarfing of the poetic and the formal as about the opening of a new philosophical importance for the medial across the 19th and 20th centuries. This new importance, as I have argued above, culminated in the new fields of media theory and media philosophy that came into their own in the mid 20th century and that have become even more influential in the human sciences subsequently. Although I tell this story largely by discussing social philosophy, I should explain that I see the rise of the medial as a more general shift in knowledge: discussing philosophy just makes the process of emergence more easily visible and traceable.

In Western philosophy, the turning point for the medial comes with Kantian philosophy, and particularly the work of Georg Wilhelm Friedrich Hegel. Before Hegel, Kantian philosophy is already suffused with strong distinctions between the poetic and the formal. There are a great many discussions of the relationship between the forces of the human spirit and of nature, of contrasting domains of the subjective and the objective throughout experience and knowledge. A fine and perhaps underrated, Kantian philosopher, Johann Gottlieb Fichte, always advised strong distinctions between a poetic domain of the human spirit (meaning for him, "activity and nothing but activity") and a formal exterior world, arguing that it was most desirable to adopt the following stance:

> All that surrounds me are mere appearances, which are present for me only insofar as I wish them to be. They are nothing to me except what I make of them myself, and they have no influence upon me except for the influence I grant them.

One could say that in Kantian philosophy more generally, the deck is stacked toward the poetic. Domains of external forms and appearances are recognized and awarded their due influence in human affairs. But, in the final analysis, they are always contingent upon human mind, will and spirit, rather than vice-versa. Likewise, the medial, for example in the case of language, is recognized as philosophically important, but principally as a manifestation of spirit or mind. This may be familiar to some of you from Protestant theology—indeed Kantian philosophy was deeply influenced by the cosmology of Pietism. So, for Johann Gottfried von Herder, another great Kantian philosopher of history (and a theologian), human language and culture are instrumental media or "blind tools" as he put it for the work of the divine Spirit in the world. The medial was thus deemed significant but largely as the instrument of the poetic (God) in the shaping of the formal (the world of creation).

Like Herder, Hegel began his intellectual career in a Pietist seminary. Giving theology up for philosophy, his contribution to the Kantian tradition is commonly acknowledged to be his centering of the dialectic of subjectivity and objectivity in his philosophical system. "Dialectic" may sound like a peculiar and technical term to you; indeed, it has brought generations of scholars to tears. But what Hegel meant by it is really not so esoteric. "Dialectic" had signaled many things in philosophy before Hegel but he redefined it specifically as a "moving principle" of the development of the world that consisted of the realization of spirit into form, the subsequent severing of spirit from form, and the cancellation of form by new extensions of spirit, all in an unceasing cycle as spirit explores its manifestations. To put it more plainly, Hegel theorized the dialectic as the internal logic of life and history, as an internal spirit extended into form, as these forms lost their spirit and were swept away by new manifestations of spirit. Hegel's dialectic suggested an endless oscillation of the poetic and the formal, perhaps not unlike Fichte's philosophy. But there was also a grander story to Hegelian philosophy. The dialectics of spirit and form served a greater purpose as the medium through which an immanent, divine Idea of self-determination, or, freedom realized itself. The realization of freedom was the task of life and history and it was the grand goal toward which everything that had happened, and which would happen, in the history of the world was oriented.

For Hegel, the Idea was also the true agent of history, using the materials of the world to accomplish its purpose; indeed, nature, all the human cultures, all human individuals and human ideas, were media of this process of the Idea's realization. Although the poetic remained the key figure in Hegel's version of the triad (after all, his dialectic of history was driven by the divine Idea and by its spirit's process of self-exploration), the medial became suddenly much more central than it had been previously in Kantian philosophy. Both the poetic and formal dimensions of nature, human lives and human cultures, were all absorbed into the project of the medial. Hegel never developed a "theory of media" in the 20th century sense but why would he bother? In good Pietist fashion, Hegel already understood everything in the world to be the medium of an immanent divine force. For our purposes, the point is that, after Hegel, the medial was here to stay.

Yet, because of the poetic power of the Idea, the medium was never "the message" for Hegel. It took Karl Marx, greatly inspired by Hegelian philosophy in his youth, to make that leap. In terms of the poetic-medial-formal triad, Marx amended Hegel's dialectical scheme in two important ways. First, he replaced the poetic of the immanent Idea with the poetic of human productive activity or "labor." With Marx, humanity, rather than a divine force, became the central agent in the development of history. Second, Marx recast the medial as a force with the capacity to exceed the force of the poetic, at least temporarily, in modern capitalist society.

To give you the punchline first, at its philosophical core, Marx's critique of capitalism identifies and attacks the medial character of modern society.

The key category for understanding Marx's vision of the medial is "capital." Marx usually defined capital negatively as "human labor in the abstract" or as the opposite of productive human activity. Capital is the quantifiable, transactable aspect of human activity, the part of us (our time and energy) that we invested into productive tasks as members of society. This sounds very curious to most contemporary readers of Marx but that is in part because Marx's insight was really rather mundane. What he was trying to capture with the term "capital" was what happened to the value of human activity when human society developed a high degree of specialized labor, an institutionalized monetary economy, and broad scales of commodity exchange. Marx saw this happening all around him as Germany began to industrialize in the first half of the 19th century, with all the social transformations that routinely accompanied early modes of industrialization—the enhanced importance of factory production, a trend toward urban migration and overcrowding, the greater rationalization of space and time both inside and outside of factories, expanded rights and institutions of private property, the normalization of wage labor and monetary economies, the efflorescence of religious movements emphasizing hard work and individual accountability (like Protestantism), and so on. These developments were clearly interrelated yet did not necessarily presuppose one another. But in the Europe of Marx's day they were something like a perfect storm, glossed together as the "Industrial Revolution" or the birth of "the modern" and their legacy has become legendary.

At the eye of the storm, Marx produced a social theory of the dynamics propelling the nascent industrial society forward, which he called "capitalism." Capitalism was foremost a problem of value for Marx; it was what happened when the objective value of human labor (think: the price of something) became more socially important than the subjective value of human labor (the value and meaning to a worker of putting his/her time and energy into producing something). Marx recognized that every society at every point in history had some kind of gap between objective value and subjective value and he called this "estrangement." But he asserted that capitalism, with its central institutions of wage labor and private property, made human estrangement total, since it reduced all or most human activity to activity oriented toward markets and money.

To understand how estrangement connects to the medial, try a small thought experiment. Think about your sneakers or, for that matter, any other thing you use routinely. Subjectively, what makes your sneakers valuable to you is their comfort, their ability to keep your feet dry and protected, and likely also the image or status they convey. But, none of these subjective needs and desires gives you a legitimate claim upon those shoes in a market-oriented society with institutionalized private property. What gives you a claim is your ability to pay their objective, market-determined price. How are you able to earn enough to buy them? Only through some other kind of activity compensated by money. Does your need for money alter even if you don't like the activity you specialize in? Sorry, no. But this seems normal since we're socialized from an early age to feel that it's impossible or at least very difficult to opt out of the monetary economy altogether.

And what are you really paying for in the price of those sneakers? It would require an enormous amount of detective work to determine that precisely but the answer would be something like: the market-determined costs of materials, labor, rent, management, machinery, storage, transport, advertising and marketing, among other inputs. None of these inputs have anything to do with your subjective need for shoes either, nor do they have much to do with the subjective value of the time and energy invested elsewhere in the making and marketing of those shoes by the suppliers of the raw materials, by the shoe assemblers, perhaps in Indonesia and China, by people involved in freighting the shoes between Asia and North America, by advertisers and marketers and sports-scientists affiliated with the sneaker company and, of course, the salespeople in the store where you purchased them.

At every link in the production chain, subjective values are coordinated by objective value, human interests and idiosyncrasies are converted into an abstract logic and language of supply, demand, price, utility, equivalence, value, and so on. One of the key effects of this continuous conversion process is that we can use routine objects like our sneakers with no sense whatsoever of the many human hands that contributed to the production, passage, and marketing of them. And, yet, without those hands, no sneakers; the other side of a complex exchange system of specialized producers is that most of us do not have the time or skill to produce useful things like sneakers for ourselves.

•••••

You see how the sneaker example confirms the common wisdom of most talk about contemporary "globalization;" how, at least when it comes to the transaction of goods and services, capitalism has made the world socially interdependent in unprecedented ways. But Marx emphasized how these interdependencies remain obscure to us—not because we are stupid or lazy—but because the scale, penetration, and complexity of markets and money (in other words, of *social mediation*) in capitalism obscure them from us. For this same reason, capitalist markets require simplified attention to the problem of value, relying typically upon quantitative, formal values rather than upon subjective, informal values. Imagine the complexity of a pricing system that really took into account what useful objects meant to all those people who were involved in their production instead of focusing on the much simpler issue of what price a buyer was willing to pay for them. An emphasis on subjective value would defeat any capitalist market as we know it, even in the age of digital information, and even though such an emphasis is not unknown to other kinds of economies, like barter and craft exchange for example, which routinely differentiate and take subjective values and interests into account.

You can also identify this phenomenon in the contemporary pressures of corporations with publicly traded stock to maintain and increase "shareholder value." What matters most to these corporations' managers are the metrics of profit and objective value monitored and determined by a now enormous, inter-national financial services industry. What matters less, especially to most metrically inclined institutional investors, is how well the company has treated its work-ers, what the company has done for society, what the subjective value of its products are to its producers and consumers, and so on. Although these are perhaps significant secondary measures of value for some companies, it is the objective, quantifiable dimension of value that is the proverbial bottom line. Marx would see this as the essence of capitalism—the centralization of markets and money, the elevation of the quantita-tive, formal side of things and therefore "estrange-ment," in human experience. In contemporary capital-ist society, like it or not, the medial sphere of exchange and transaction reigns supreme, utilizing the formal, objective dimension of value to triumph over the poetic, and, for Marx, "human" dimension of value.

If, in Marx's critique of capitalism, the medial really does become the message of history, it does so only temporarily. Marx saw capitalism as a kind of necessary evil in human history lodged between early modes of production and institutions of exploitative estrangement (like slavery in Greek and Roman civilization and serfdom under feudalism) and an inevitable transcendence of estrangement after the overthrow of capitalism. Here Marx had more in common with Hegel than he would have liked to admit. The concluding chapter of Marx's philosophy of history predicted the restoration of the poetic in history in a triumphant new era of human self-determination which would follow a communist revolution. Marx believed (romantically or irrationally many critics contend) it was inevitable that humanity would eventually rise against capital since capitalism created the conditions for its own demise. Capital unified humanity as never before by situating them as wage laborers in a global exchange system and by exploiting them relentlessly in order to maximize profit. Marx predicted that this newly unified, self-aware humanity would eventually seek to elevate its subjective interests over those of capital. In the end, we could expect from a post-capitalist world something approximating Hegel's Idea of freedom, but without God and in the name of humanity alone.

So, Marx's philosophy of history eventually restored the poetic to prominence, making the empire of the medial (e.g., capitalism) into a transitory phase in the course of human history. It was unthinkable to Marx that the medial could dominate human history forever. And, yet, over the remainder of the 19th and 20th centuries, the horizonless dominance of the medial increasingly became common wisdom among philosophers and social theorists. On the one hand, this was the era that gave birth to modern utilitarian paradigms in economics that enshrined market logics of production and consumption, supply and demand in the core of human character. On the other, in European artistic and literary culture of the late 19th century, for example, it was very common to hear criticism of the overformalization of modern society and of a plague of "mass culture" (meaning mass media) and technical, specialized knowledge that cheapened and corrupted the poetic powers of true culture and genius. Mass culture was said to make mass humans, each interchangeable with all the others. Friedrich Nietzsche was perhaps the greatest poet of such sentiment, indicting the modern "last man," the epitome of mediocrity and herd mentality, with brilliant rhetorical flourishes. The advance of the domain of the medial seemed unstoppable in the late 19th century, auguring a cultural collapse into an atomized, market- and state-determined humanity. The prospect led some to advocate radical, even millenarian, solutions to reawaken a poetic force in history—whether the force of philosophy and science, or nationalism, or the proletariat, or youth—with the power to reverse the advance of the medial and to return its powers again to human purposes.

It is important to understand that early media theory took shape in this climate, in the shadow of crystallizing certainty about the monolithic power of the medial in modern society. It emerged in political movements (like Lenin's theory of propaganda) and in intellectual circles (like the Frankfurt School's cultural criticism of mass culture and new media like photography, film, and radio) which sought to restore the poetic to prominence in human history, whether through social revolution, artistic experimentation or scientific progress. Unlike McLuhan, early media theory tended to resist treating mass communication as an autonomous force in human social experience, preferring to link the power of media instead to the historical force of capitalism or modernity. The Frankfurt School critic, Walter Benjamin, who was probably more attentive to the properties and powers of media than any of his contemporaries, still wrote that the character of the medium was ultimately determined by history and not vice-versa.

The shift to the medium as the message of history came, as we have heard, only with McLuhan. And, McLuhan was also a powerful expression of the now unquestioned importance of the medial in Western philosophy—in some ways, it's remarkable that it took so long for someone to make the argument for the dominance of the medial as blatantly as McLuhan did since there had been so many flirtations with it since Hegel and Marx. Such perhaps is the tenacity of our faith in the poetic (and/or the formal).

McLuhan's was clearly not a voice crying in the wilderness, however. Part of what the recent McLuhan renaissance has recognized is that McLuhan's media theory bore striking resemblance to other theories of mediation that emerged, particularly in France, in the

1960s. Media theorist Friedrich Kittler has noted, for example, that McLuhan's language of media extensions is not far removed from the language of *pouvoir* (power, or better, "enablement") that historian and philosopher Michel Foucault developed in his analysis of modern society. The new mode of sociality that McLuhan predicts for the electric era is really quite similar in its contours to Foucault's general diagnosis of modernity, which emphasized the suffusion of human experience with new military, medical, penal, juridical, aesthetic, economic, and scientific technologies of power. Like McLuhan's cybernetic understanding of media, Foucault's cybernetic understanding of power limits the significance of both the poetic powers of humanity and the formal powers of the object world, revealing all to be nothing other than assemblages of medial forces and technologies. Elsewhere, at roughly the same time, the sociological systems theory developed by Niklas Luhmann offers a very similar portrait of medial-technical assemblages, or, "systems" that create and interlink our social, psychological and biological environments. More recently, a "posthuman" movement has swept across the humanities and social sciences in the 1990s from actor-network theory to cyborg theory. Yet, the subtleties of theoretical difference aside, all these cases share something in common: they center their philosophies in metaphors of the medial—assemblages, capital, flows, hybrids, matrices, networks, rhizomes, systems, etc. All make mediation the message of ontology and epistemology.

Although Foucaultian, Luhmannian and other medial philosophy have all had tremendous resonance in academic culture over the past twenty-five years, it would be inaccurate to argue that all contemporary philosophy emphasizes the dominance of the medial. It doesn't. The importance of the poetic and the formal has not been neglected and both still have many proponents, including this author, even though medial philosophy does seem to have claimed for itself the role of avant-garde and prophecy of the future. But, by positioning itself as a fresh burst of truth, much contemporary medial philosophy is unable to acknowledge the depth of its tradition and its slow development to plausibility across the 19th and 20th centuries and unwilling to provide a careful archaeology of its attentions and interests. No, as I said at the beginning, this story has not been of the death or diminishment of the poetic and the formal so much as it has been about the expansion of attention to, and valuation of, the medial in human experience. Knowledge is intrinsically expansive and excessive; it makes no sense to study it as a zero sum game.

What does the medial message?

After this long philosophical digest, you are doubtless still left pondering the most important question: why the medial, what does its gradual rise to prominence in knowledge mean? This is the kind of question whose answer will inevitably be too detailed or too simplistic. Given my limited space and your taxed patience, I'll opt for the latter. For, like most things having to do with philosophy, the phenomenon itself is less complicated than its technical language of expression would make it seem.

The poetic-medial-formal triad in knowledge is largely, in my understanding of it, a division and special-ization of attentions. It is a way of conceptually orga-nizing and specifying the origin point of forces at work in the world. Put simply, the poetic is attention to the capacity we human beings have for producing, making, doing things. It reflects our awareness of our capacity to bring forth, to create changes in our environments. We are certain of the existence of the poetic principally because we are active subjects in the world and we can believe that our activity is the result of ordained-from-above will, ontological accident, or that the only thing that matters is the experience of activity in the world itself. The formal meanwhile is attention to externality (and, especially, external forms), to the existence in our lives of things and forces that are not-us. This some-times even extends to those parts of ourselves that are gendered distinct from our spiritual-mental core like our bodies. And, we can believe that we determine externality or that externalities determine us or that we co-determine each other and in every case we will see the formal as an important dimension of human experi-ence. The medial, it seems to me, is attention to the experience of transaction and translocation, put more plainly, to phenomena like language and exchange and tools and movement, to the middle-grounds and means of human life. As I noted above, at various points in the history of philosophy, non-Western as well as Western, the medial may be conjoined more or less closely with the poetic and the formal in ways that are hopefully now clearer. What still requires clarification is why, in the Western tradition we have reviewed, the ratio of attentions shifted to the point that the medial could be apprehended as fully autonomous of the poetic and the formal and, indeed, in some cases, as determining the poetic and the formal.

Here, I would turn back to Marx again, not to the technical substance of his social theory, but to the gist of what motivated him in the first place to produce his analysis and criticism of the medial dimension of modern life. What Marx saw as the defining condition of modernity was *social mediation*, the expansion and coordination of instruments, spaces, and institutions of transaction. It's not as though there was no mediation before modernity nor that with modernity immediate relations between human subjects and their useful objects ceased. Marx's vision was one of shifting proportions. He captured how producing and acquiring useful things became an increasingly abstract, complex and energy-consuming enterprise in the era he termed "capitalism," involving networks and relations of production and exchange that, in some cases, spanned continents. To manage the increasing scale and complexity of exchange, institutions and instruments of transaction (like wage labor, markets, money, and private property) inevitably became proportionally more important and influential in human experience.

This, I think, was Marx's most important insight—the tipping of the scales from the qualitative and immediate into the quantitative and mediate as the hallmark of modernity. Marx didn't stop here, of course, he went on to argue with polemical zeal—but inaccurately I believe—that the medial exerted a universally solvent, exploitative effect under capitalism, making humans slaves to the social system of production and reducing all culture to prostitution and imitation. The simplicity of the story is probably what has made it so compelling to generations of poeticist and formalist critics of the medial since Marx. But the history of humanity under capitalism has been more than the ascendancy of market rationality, involving a plurality of beliefs, interests, practices and valuations, others of which are clearly transactional in their character, some of which might legitimately be labeled "crypto-transactional" in their orientation, yet some of which can also not be fairly reduced to transactional logics and market orientations. For example, capitalism has never dispelled entirely actions inspired by human sympathy and interest in the welfare of others, nor has it reduced all meaningful human relations to market relations, nor has it eradicated modes of cultural creativity not reducible to self-interest or market-interest. Marx's relative inattention to the stubborn plurality of human immediacies and non-market mediations under capitalism is perhaps the strength of his political rhetoric but it is also the weak link in his critical theory.

The better argument we can develop from Marx is historical, that Western industrialism, exploration, trade, and imperialism, across the 18th, 19th and 20th centuries, gradually rather than suddenly, catalyzed expanded attention to the medial. Not in the same way or at the same rate everywhere and perhaps in some cases at the expense of attention to the poetic or the formal, but not in any absolute sense. The point is that the expanded transactional sphere produced ripples in human knowledge and culture wherever it developed. But Western cultures were not made homogeneously utilitarian, nor were non-Western cultures swept away or assimilated—but each, in some way, developed a greater attention to transactional and translocational forces. And, with greater attention, came a sense of rising proportional importance and power for the medial in human affairs. One can see this, for example, in the proliferation of new cultural forms across the world in the 19th and 20th centuries that focused on the power of the medial yet, like Melanesian cargo cults, sought to tame these forces by also reincorporating them into cultural traditions. Anthropologists have documented countless cases of other cultural practices—ranging from movements of religious salvation, to concern with hauntings, witchcraft, and spectral visitations, to cultural revivalism and heritage movements, to ethnic essentialism and sectarian violence—that recognize and respond to, in some way, a sense of the heightened presence of the medial in contemporary life. To this inventory of cultural responses, we should also add Western medial philosophy, everyday talk of "the media" and "the market" and not least Marx's restless critique of capital itself.

It is important to note that many of these cultural practices not only recognize medial forces but also seek to temper them. Many treat the medial as a source of unsettling power and offer ways of reasserting the countervailing presence of poetic and/or formal forces, if only by locating a remediable source or cause of medial power in a particular person (like a witch) or in a particular group of persons (like the Jews in Nazi Europe) or in a particular class of objects (like modern technology). But why should the medial inspire such concern? Although the cultural phenomena in question are too various to distill down to a single root cause, I suspect the unease has something to do with the elusiveness of the medial in the first place, with an inability to define clearly where "middle-grounds" and "means" end and the more experientially secure domains of the poetic and the formal (the domains of the "I" and the "not-I") begin. A seemingly autonomous medial sphere may also destabilize our sense of a stable governing order or structure of accountability in human affairs (whether of human, natural or divine origin) that is not simply a matter of flows, motion, transaction, and so on. In scholarly life, we observe such concerns, for example, in anxious discourse surrounding a so-called "postmodern turn" or "dilemma" besetting post-1960s culture and society. But what such talk about radical social and cultural change orbits is the real dilemma of how to establish what anthropologist Michael Jackson has termed "ontological security" in a world that seems as complexly interdependent, transactional and mediated as our does. We fear that the expansion of the medial means domination by the medial. And we wonder: mustn't we just embrace contingency (or deny it through absolutism) instead?

••••

But, please, let's not sound so apocalyptic. We should remind ourselves that social mediation has always challenged our ability to know its forms and forces. There is nothing particularly new about that. Social mediation, whether truly global or operating as it more often does on a much more limited scale, challenges social knowledge; it always reminds us of the relational, interdependent, contingent character of what we do and what we know. Social mediation offers many tantalizing hints of persons, relations, forces and objects beyond the certainty of what is known to us experientially. Yet they, their agency, their patterns of cause and effect, are usually unknowable in their totality. Still, as noted at the outset, we reason across such gaps in experiential certainty all the time, modeling forces and relations we don't understand upon ones that we do or think we do. So, one common way of conceptualizing social mediation is to translate these hints into impression that medial forces circulate according to their own interests and logics. Thus, McLuhan. Another is to translate the perceived power of the medial into more personified or technicized images, whether into belief in the companion presence of intervening, mediating spirits like Djinn or into belief in the power of technical artifacts like the printing press to change the world. Both moves secure a conceptually clear agent for social mediation, making uncertain, even anxiety-inducing, medial forces appear more familiar and mundane.

If the first half of this essay has analyzed the heightened attention to media and the medial in modern western culture, then what I would like to demonstrate in the second half of this essay is the deep traction that poetic and formal understandings retain in our common habits of thinking and talking about media. *Even if more attention is paid to the message of mediation these days, it is striking that poetic and formal modes of understanding media are just as routine.* I explore how the core certainties we have about media often *immediate the medial,* that is, they temper the expansive and excessive qualities of social mediation by treating media as instruments of human creative powers or as technologies, technical forms with an intrinsic, objective set of qualities and capacities. Thinking back to my characterization of the poetic, the medial and the formal as specializations of attention, this should not be too surprising. Specialized attentions deepen knowledge of one domain or aspect of experience but in so doing they create blind spots elsewhere, which, in turn, may become the foci of other specialized attentions. Specialized attentions are thus intrinsically complementary to one another. The complementarity of poetic, medial, and formal certainties regarding media is the focus of the remainder of this essay.

II

Media Instruments,
Media Technologies, Media Excess

In the first part of this section, with the help of case studies, I'd like to explore three certainties we have managed to achieve about what media are and what they do. These studies help to show in a much more practical way how our habits of understanding media recognize the power of social mediation but how they also typically immediate media, dampening down the medial qualities of media, and drawing our thinking and talking about media into the orbit of poetic and formal certainties. Put plainly, despite all the media hype, all the talk of the excess and power of mediation, we still commonly grasp media either poetically as inert instruments of human purposes or formally as technologies, technical forms with intrinsic powers of their own.

Thus, these three certainties will not seem extraordinary to you, rather probably very mundane. But, truly, what could be more influential in knowledge than what is taken for granted? The first certainty is that *media are messaging instruments,* that is, tools or conduits for communication between persons or between persons and other kinds of social entities. We explore this certainty through the case of telephony. The second certainty is that *media are technologies of information and communication,* that is, formal technologies with objective technical capacities (of data circulation, management and storage, for example) that shape human social action. We explore this certainty through the case of the internet. The third certainty is that *media are vehicles of cultural expression,* means of articulating and defining human culture. We explore this certainty through the case of televisual media and debates over their cultural influence. If the first case focuses on poetic understanding and the second case on formal understanding then the third case shows how poetic and formal modes of understanding media are by no means exclusive; each is intimately intertwined with the other in actual situations of media talk and media thinking, just as both are intertwined with medial understandings of media. All three modes of understanding are *fundamentally complementary* to each other. They are all present in how we understand any medium. The key questions are: in what proportion and why?

As discussed in the last section, our contemporary experience of media occurs against the backdrop of profound social mediation. And, yet, to listen to the knowledge we have created about media, you wouldn't always know it: our habits of understanding media certainly do not always emphasize the medial. I think immediation is often desirable, especially in contemporary western societies, simply as a reaction to the depth and presence of modes of social mediation around us. But lack of attention to the medial can also be explained more directly in many cases because the experience of utilizing some media has become relatively *contained*. Case in point: the telephone.

Talking wires

Say you are itching to tell a friend about something that just happened. You pick up a telephone, what could be easier? You dial a number into a keypad and a connection is sought, a phone rings in your friend's house or pocket, the connection is completed, and *voilà*, you and your friend are offered a real-time communicative situation within which you can deliver your message. A human agent (you) has exercised her or his will to send a message, has sought a device of messaging at hand, and, the message is transmitted to a second agent (your friend). This agent-instrument-agent series is a very common, perhaps even the most common, way of understanding media communication. After all, when it comes to the experience of a medium like telephony we often focus less on the medium itself then on our guiding intention (for example, to make a call or to deliver a message). Little wonder then that the medium easily slips into the role of a tool, a *messaging instrument*, that allows us to realize that intention.

So what's wrong with this understanding? Up to a point, nothing, really. There's nothing incorrect in thinking about a telephone as an instrument or in the service of a human purpose. For one thing, everyday experience of these useful devices validates that understanding. For another, from its very beginning, this was the inspiration for the telephone. Alexander Graham Bell, an elocutionist by family background and training, was taken with the idea of producing a "musical telegraph" or "talking wire" that would allow for direct human speech across great distances, unmediated by the abstract codings of telegraphy. The very first advertisement for a telephone in 1877 put the case for its improvement upon telegraphy thus:

1. No skilled operator is required, but direct communication may be had by speech without the intervention of a third person.

2. The communication is much more rapid, the average number of words transmitted in a minute by the Morse sounder being from fifteen to twenty, by telephone from one to two hundred.

3. No expense is required, either for its operation or repair. It needs no battery and has no complicated machinery. It is unsurpassed for economy and simplicity.

So, one could argue that the telephone was always imagined to function in the way we routinely assume it to function, that is, as a communicative instrument "unsurpassed for economy and simplicity."

But what must also be considered are the enormous labors of invention and maintenance that historically contributed to making telephony such a routine and unproblematic companion instrument. This is why I would say that understanding the telephone as a messaging instrument is not a wrong understanding, it's a limited, specialized understanding, one that's tailored to immediate experience of the medium and less attentive to its full history of social and technological development.

If you read Herbert Casson's delightful 1910 book, *The History of the Telephone*, for example, you immediately get a sense of how much early telephony differed from our contemporary experience. The basic technology (a sound signal carried across an electric wire) was not so different from the telephony I grew up with in the 1970s. But, in its early years, seemingly the most essential aspect of telephony, the direct communication of human voice, was contingent upon cabling that was unable to shield invasive signals, creating an impressive cacophony as Casson reports:

> Noises! Such a jangle of meaningless noises had never been heard by human ears. There were spluttering and bubbling, jerking and rasping, whistling and screaming. There were the rustling of leaves, the croaking of frogs, the hissing of steam, and the flapping of birds' wings. There were clicks from telegraph wires, scraps of talk from other telephones, and curious little squeals that were unlike any known sound. The lines running east and west were noisier than the lines running north and south. The night was noisier than the day, and at the ghostly hour of midnight, for what strange reason no one knows, the babel was at its height. ...[T]he matter-of-fact young telephonists agreed to lay the blame on "induction"—a hazy word

which usually meant the natural meddlesomeness of electricity.

Our present telephonic menu of well-shielded copper cables, fiber optics, and, increasingly, broadband and wireless technologies has rendered such interference increasingly unfamiliar in wealthier countries. But some of you may recall from your own lifetimes the ghostly visitation of "crossed cables," picking up a phone only to discover another call already in progress. Or, a little further back, the *Pillow Talk*-esque adventures and misadventures of party lines.

Furthermore, the present telephonic instrument derives a good part of its character from fully automated electronic switching systems which were introduced only after the early 1960s. Until this technical development, direct communication was much rarer and placing a call usually required the further mediation of a switchboard operator, a job that invites comparisons to an air-traffic controller in terms of its speed and pressure. Again, Casson:

> To describe one of those early telephone exchanges in the silence of a printed page is a wholly impossible thing. Nothing but a language of noise could convey the proper impression. An editor who visited the Chicago exchange in 1879 said of it: "The racket is almost deafening. Boys are rushing madly hither and thither, while others are putting in or taking out pegs from a central framework as if they were lunatics engaged in a game of fox and geese." In the same year E. J. Hall wrote from Buffalo that his exchange with twelve boys had become "a perfect Bedlam." By the clumsy methods of those

days, from two to six boys were needed to handle each call. And as there was usually more or less of a cat-and-dog squabble between the boys and the public, with every one yelling at the top of his voice, it may be imagined that a telephone exchange was a loud and frantic place. Boys, as operators, proved to be most complete and consistent failures. Their sins of omission and commission would fill a book. What with whittling the switchboards, swearing at subscribers, playing tricks with the wires, and roaring on all occasions like young bulls of Bashan, the boys in the first exchanges did their full share in adding to the troubles of the business.... Like the MYSTERIOUS NOISES they could not be controlled, and by general consent they were abolished. In place of the noisy and obstreperous boy came the docile, soft-voiced girl.

On the one hand, the telephone exchange was a technical apparatus but it was also an entire social world, filled with its own internal communications, organizational hierarchies, gender relations and stereotypes, forms of expertise, and so on. To complete successfully the simple and efficient action of making a phone call and delivering a message an entire social world had to be involved, its technology solicited, its organization navigated and its inhabitants confronted (in some cases, confronted aggressively).

     Although our mode of engagement is now more technically mediated and remote, all this remains true of telephony today. Such a claim may sound odd given the apparent transparency of using a telephone. It's true that Casson's exchanges are places of the past, but other social and technical infrastructures have developed to replace them, infrastructures upon which present-day telephony is equally dependent to control its "mysterious noises" and "natural meddlesomeness." Cable is in the ground all around us, telephone call centers abound, as do cellular towers (in some cases imaginatively disguised as everything from church steeples to trees). U.S. Department of Labor statistics estimated that there were over one million jobs in the telecommunications industry in 2004 in the U.S. alone, ranging from sales to installation to computer systems design and maintenance. Without this support system of specialists, organizations, and technical infrastructure, the contemporary experience of telephony as direct communication would be unsustainable, or, at least, far more rife with environmental "noise" than it is. The vision, even the technology, on its own guarantees very little, as Bell and other telephonic pioneers realized over a century ago.

Acknowledging the social mediation present in telephony of course takes nothing away from its experiential streamlining. Telephony is both a wondrously simple and surprisingly flexible enterprise nowadays. Not only has the switching become fully automated but the services and platforms are expanding. There are prophets of a "Next Generation Network" who already foresee telephony as a free service fully integrated with the internet and its digital "packet-switching" system. As they note, glimpses of this future are already here. It's a fair bet that some of you now buy digital phone service from your cable television provider, some of you routinely use VoIP (voice over internet protocol) software like Skype that can convert your computer into a phone, and some of you have given up your land-lines for cell-phones. With the iPhone the much anticipated fusion of computer and phone into a single device has taken a great leap forward. But that's just the cutting edge. Even for those with no interest in "next generation" telephony, phones are cheap, reliable and durable, lines are easy to come by and, as long as you stay on the right side of the regime, uninterfered with. Service can be set up within a matter of days and it takes a serious electrical problem or a major storm to knock it out, and then only temporarily. The experiential bottom line is that for those wealthy and well-positioned enough to acquire the relevant technologies, infrastructure and expertise, we seem to have largely attained Bell's dream of a simple and efficient instrument that permits direct communication of the human voice with minimal outside influence and interference. It's no wonder that it is profoundly easy for people like us to experience telephony instrumentally.

Yet, this quintessential experience of media instrumentality is also remarkably fragile. Social and technical projects of immediation often successfully dampen experiential recognition of the medial and formal dimensions of media but they also remain perpetually unfulfilled, even in cases like telephony, where they have achieved a great deal. The truth of the matter is that telephony *is* interrupted, phones malfunction, VoIP in moments of peak bandwidth usage is undermined by packet delays, we walk into a building and lose our cellular signal, and so on. In these moments, the otherwise very persuasive and compelling experience of the domesticated instrument is momentarily interrupted by the recurrence of medial and/or formal concerns.

Such interruptions are also widely anticipated in the rich life of media fantasy. A good example from film is how the unexpected phone call has long served as an ominous portent, from Hitchcock to *The Ring*. Why does it send shivers up our spine? Because the unexpected phone call is a concrete reminder of the limits of immediating media, that even domesticated messaging instruments like the telephone retain a medial capacity to channel uninvited messages "from beyond." What's most uncomfortable, indeed creepy, about the unexpected phone call is not the caller, not even the message, but just that we have been located by someone or *something*—the telephone thus becomes an index for the arrival of mysterious powers from afar. The fantasy of being imperiled by the phone seems rather apt given how many of us feel and talk these days as though we are enslaved by the convenience of cellular telephony. We carry our phones with us everywhere, making us always available to receive messages, both invited and uninvited. And, when was the last time you were at a public gathering and someone's cellphone *didn't* make an intrusion? We all know it's going to happen, yet it still delivers an unpleasant shock, sending us scrambling to make sure we're not the guilty parties. Projects of immediation are designed to minimize such experiential moments of unexpected and uncontrolled mediation, making the medium as contained and tool-like as possible. With the telephone, this has worked reasonably well—the average telephone call now seems like nothing more than a happy union of human intentions and technological capacities. But what happens in our experience of other media, ones lacking the handy, portable material form of a phone or in which a density of transactional and translocational forces seems to be their primary experiential feature? Interestingly, here as well we find that it is possible to immediate the medial. Case in point: the internet.

Backbone of the information society

Now, if the internet isn't a medial medium, I don't know what is. Over a billion users worldwide, over four hundred million hosts, who knows how many websites, a global network of interconnected routers managing data flows measured in gigabytes/second, terabytes/day, moving across the world in spans of time marked by milliseconds. Here's a sobering thought: no one, not even experts in internet architecture and traffic, really knows exactly how big the internet is, or, how many people are using it at a given time. The distributed networks of interlinked computers that compose the internet have developed to a degree of complexity and abundance that currently exceeds even our most technically astute methods of assessment. And, this is not even to mention spam, popups, blind links, viruses, zombies, cookies, bots, and all the other daily reminders of the medial swirl of the internet. If you had to pick one medium that epitomizes the excess of social mediation in our day and age, it would have to be the internet, this wired mass of oceanic, near instantaneous transaction, spanning every continent.

And, surely, the medial character of the internet has not gone unnoticed, especially in popular culture. Can you imagine a more vivid portrait of the medial then *The Matrix* series of films—Marx would have been proud—with their fantasy of a computer network whose extractive and creative powers have come to exceed vastly those of its human progenitors (even if, in the final act, the poetic reemerges triumphant)? Less self-important and noir is comedian Dave Chappelle's routine where he reflects on what the internet would look like if it were an actual, physical space and imagines a seedy, chaotic shopping mall, traversed by countless rushing consumers, navigating thieves, pushy salespeople, and illicit propositions. Without downplaying the significance of medial fantasies and anxieties of the internet, whether expressed in Hollywood film or in everyday life, the medial dimension of the internet is actually less highlighted these days then one would have any reasonable right to expect given what the internet is and has become.

In most Western countries, the heyday of medial thinking about new electronic information and communication technologies (or "ICTs" in the lingo) actually came in the late 1990s, the heart of the McLuhan renaissance, with the saturation of public culture with rhetoric of ICT-driven social revolution. We heard countless experts, trembling with conviction, explain that new media were changing everything. We heard of a new regime of digital connectivity and instantaneity was poised to unsettle the habits and conventions of the "bricks and mortar" world. Soon most commerce would be transacted on-line, most communication would be digital, our homes, vehicles and bodies would be equipped and enhanced by information technologies, new virtual modes of civic engagement would replace old institutions, and so on. Ideas, habits, institutions would be forced to adapt tout court to these new extensional powers. Although disconcerting to many, this transformation was often painted in a positive light. With all this innovation afoot, with so much ICT-enhanced productivity abroad, the mood was positively emancipatory. Even the old empire of the medial, capitalism, seemed to lose its mysteries, its exploitation, its riskiness. Internet trading meant that it was easy to participate and the high-flying tech stock market meant that everyone could profit.

The old empire wagered a lot of investment capital that these social changes would take place more or less immediately. They didn't. Unproven internet start-up firms were taken public and showered in financing without having produced a penny of profit. A few among these, like Amazon, eventually rewarded their investors, while countless others like Webvan burned through hundreds of millions of dollars before collapse. The ill-starred AOL Time Warner merger of 2001 marked both the culmination and the collapse of new media mania. With its typical penchant for sharp satire, *The Onion* ran a news-bulletin the week after the merger announcement, "AOL Acquires Time Warner In Largest-Ever Expenditure Of Pretend Internet Money." In 2002, AOL Time Warner posted a 99 billion dollar loss, at the time the largest loss ever posted by a company.

But it wasn't just the pyramidal thinking of a market bubble that prompted such medial faith in the social power of the internet and ICTs more generally. No one would have bought into the ICT stock pyramids if they hadn't already believed that media were the message, that they were changing our social worlds in ways we could scarcely understand because everything was happening *so fast*. Such sentiments weren't novel in the late 1990s, of course; McLuhan and others had made similar prophecies concerning electronic media since the 1960s. But, meanwhile, other modes of social mediation had also extended their scales and influence. The internationalization of trade, finance, war and development in the 1960s and 1970s helped set the stage for the decline of state-oriented Keynesian economic programs and the rise of aggressive liberalization and marketization policies in many parts of the world. The political trend we call "neoliberalism" today, with its ideological opposition to the sovereignty and legitimacy of states to regulate market interests, took shape during this period. The final act of postwar geopolitics—the collapse of the Soviet bloc in 1989—was accompanied by much talk of victory for capitalism, predictions of global free trade and liberal democracy, and, not least, "the end of history."

So, long before the talk of digital revolution in the late 1990s, much of the ideological groundwork for ideas of radical transformation via social mediation had already been laid. Social theorist Arjun Appadurai described global culture in the late 1980s, for example, as a landscape of "disjuncture and difference" typified by unsettling juxtapositions, from vast new waves of labor migration to the sampling and hybridity of pop cultures across the world. All these developments contributed to the message of the medial—the sense of emergent transactional and translocational powers and profoundly mediated lives. Some celebrated these powers, including many who had the resources and knowledge to benefit from the internationalization of finance and markets. Others galvanized against them, seeking to master the medial perhaps through religion or political action. The 1980s and 1990s were not incidentally also a growth period for new forms of religious conservatism, anti-globalization movements, culture wars, and so on.

●●●●

One could argue that "disjuncture and difference" still describes the dominant trends of global culture today. But I think it is also fair to say that talk about the internet has meanwhile developed a more sedate and richly formal understanding of the medium, one that has shifted focus away from mysterious medial powers and toward technical properties. Chief among the noted properties remains digital instantaneity, the power of communicational immediacy believed intrinsic to ICTs. In essence, this same sense of immediacy saturated much medial talk and thinking as well. But there it was a rampant power, not one that could be subject to any principle of control or guidance other than its own excessive transactional logic. The difference with the

shift in emphasis from a medial to a formal understanding is that the internet and other ICTs have come
to be identified as intrinsically powerful yet also
manageable technologies of information and communication. Even if no one pretends that the internet is a
kind of domesticated messaging tool like the telephone, aspects of it (like the use of email) are rather
contained. Moreover, in their entirety, ICTs are treated
as a formal network, potent but holding no intrinsic
agenda of its own, and thus open to leveraging by
human agents for a variety of social purposes.

So, for every critic of internet pornography and
apocalypt of the end of privacy in the information age
we find a Nicholas Negroponte or Lawrence Lessig
championing the internet's capacity to overturn social,
economic and political inequalities throughout the
world. Consider, for example, the World Summit on
the Information Society's recent (2005) Tunis
Commitment, which includes a number of statements
of the following spirit:

> ICTs are making it possible for a vastly larger popu-
> lation than at any time in the past to join in sharing
> and expanding the base of human knowledge, and
> contributing to its further growth in all spheres of
> human endeavour as well as its application to educa-
> tion, health and science.

> We underscore that ICTs are effective tools to
> promote peace, security and stability, to enhance
> democracy, social cohesion, good governance and
> the rule of law, at national, regional and interna-
> tional levels.

We hear that ICTs archive and share human knowledge to an unprecedented degree, that they create new kinds of connectedness and opportunities, thus, according to WSIS, "laying the groundwork for the establishment of a fully inclusive and development-oriented Information Society and knowledge economy which respects cultural and linguistic diversity."

Such statements are persuasive to many of us. It is certainly not a radical position to suggest that ICTs are "effective tools" and that they are "laying the groundwork" for a new information-centered society. So, what has allowed us to immediate the medial here? How is possible to sustain the image of this massive open network of mediation as a tool or technology that can be put to service to promote peace, enhance democracy, and so on? Experientially, what needs to be highlighted is that ICTs like email and the internet have, in fact, opened remarkable new communicative possibilities for elite and educated social strata across the world over the past fifteen years. In these social strata, and among many professional groups, it is quite fair to describe ICTs as revolutionary. Financial services industries have expanded and benefited enormously from the availability of "real-time" market information from around the world. One could argue that finance's social power has increased so exponentially in recent decades because it enjoys the tactical advantage of global networking and coordination over hundreds of uncoordinated (or less coordinated) governments. News journalism has also changed significantly owing to new digital information technologies; texts and images can circulate around the world with astonishing speed creating a kind of "global village" effect. On the other hand, many journalists and critics feel that news diversity has actually decreased because it no longer makes sense for most news organizations to invest heavily in costly correspondent networks producing original news because any "scoop" will be picked up by wire services organizations and made available digitally to every other news organization in the world in a matter of minutes. To offer a more personal example, the speed and flexibility of email has allowed me to work on extensive collaborative projects with scholars in Africa, Australia and Europe over the past ten years. The internet's archive has even saved me from setting foot in a library in the writing of this text. Of course, I could have made these connections and done this research and writing before the popularization of email and internet, but digital media have been wonderfully enabling in my profession as I am sure they have been enabling to you as well. Doesn't it seem logical then to conclude that, over the long run, these technologies could work their technical magic elsewhere as well, spreading democracy and opportunity, relieving poverty and undermining tyranny?

One should be at least a little skeptical of media understandings that generalize personal experience, or the experience of one's social stratum and place, to the world. The triumphant one-world networked future imagined by WSIS looks past the profound inequities in media access across the world and talks around the necessity of a one-world social and technical infrastructure that took decades to develop even in the wealthy West, involving the establishment of conduits (e.g., cabling, fiber optics, broadband and wireless technology), the industrial production of computers and servers, the development and standardization of both a digital packet-switching network and protocols (e.g., TCP/IP) to allow computers to communicate with each other, the institutionalization of agencies to coordinate the network (e.g., the U.S.-based ICANN), and, just as importantly, the expansion of specialized technical education required to sell, service, maintain, adapt and operate these technologies and the cultivation of communities of professional and non-professional specialists invested in working with ICTs.

What the Tunis Commitment does capture very well is the social experience of ICTs by the international elite professional caste who also populate the WSIS. When they speak of a nascent "Information Society" organized around the backbone of ICTs, they are anchoring their futurology in the new speeds, means, utilities, and scales of social connectedness that ICTs have already made available to people like them. This is the experiential basis of the heightened formal understanding of the internet among social elites across the world. For them, and they (we) would say, for everyone, ICTs offer not only wonderful communicative tools like email but also offer more generally a technical environment whose properties enable social projects of information and communication at hitherto unknown scales and speeds.

It is worth noting that, just like the vision of the telephone as a messaging instrument, the vision of the internet as a technical apparatus of knowledge management has accompanied it from its earliest imaginings.

What is less often acknowledged is that the social project of information technology was also a reaction to concerns with the medial character of modern knowledge. The first image of the internet is usually credited to the man who directed the United States Office of Scientific Research and Development during World War II, Vannevar Bush, an electrical engineer by training. Bush not only helped set up research programs during and after WWII that would contribute much of the science and technical inventions necessary for the internet but he also provided the first popular description of an internet-like device, the "memex," in a July, 1945 article for *The Atlantic Monthly*.

Bush's text has been canonized in internet scholarship for his brief but evocative description of the memex ("a device in which an individual stores all his books, records, and communications, and which is mechanized so that it may be consulted with exceeding speed and flexibility"). And, yet, the vast majority of Bush's article was actually devoted to considering the Nietzschean problem of human knowledge in an era in which the bounty of specialized scientific research seems increasingly overwhelming:

> There is a growing mountain of research. But there is increased evidence that we are being bogged down today as specialization extends. The investigator is staggered by the findings and conclusions of thousands of other workers—conclusions which he cannot find time to grasp, much less to remember, as they appear. Yet specialization becomes increasingly necessary for progress, and the effort to bridge between disciplines is correspondingly superficial.

Unlike Nietzsche, Bush was not seeking a revolutionary or romantic transcendence of specialized knowledge, quite the contrary, but he was acutely aware that our instruments of managing knowledge were not keeping pace with the social specialization of scientific research and with the abundance and complexity of specialized knowledge being produced. Alert to the dangers of this situation for steady scientific progress, he also saw enormous opportunities were this abundance of specialized knowledge to be better archived and sorted.

For this reason, Bush didn't imagine the memex exclusively as a memory device or archive. He also explicitly considered it as a device for selection and for forgetting, thus reducing the pressure of the increasing abundance of knowledge upon the relatively stable capacities of human memory. The penultimate paragraph of Bush's essay reads:

> Presumably man's spirit should be elevated if he can better review his shady past and analyze more completely and objectively his present problems. He has built a civilization so complex that he needs to mechanize his records more fully if he is to push his experiment to its logical conclusion and not merely become bogged down part way there by overtaxing his limited memory. His excursions may be more enjoyable if he can reacquire the privilege of forgetting the manifold things he does not need to have immediately at hand, with some assurance that he can find them again if they prove important.

Bush's message, to put it in other words, was that we needed new technical prosthetics for managing the vast and growing abundance of human knowledge, which he viewed as much as a bog as a library. In 1945 no one was talking about "ICTs" let alone the internet, yet what Bush's article teaches us is that managing the medial has always been the premise of the social project of creating new information technology (e.g., developing "effective tools" like the internet). Information technology is not just about guaranteeing an abundance of knowledge, but about limiting it. And, it is also about limiting what can be technically defined as knowledge. A few years later, in 1948, one of Bush's former students at MIT, Claude Shannon, published an essay, "A Mathematical Theory of Communication," that is widely credited with codifying a new field of applied mathematics, information theory. Research on the mathematics of communication, which co-evolved with computer science and cybernetics between the 1930s and 1950s, shared these fields' interest in the development and refinement of algorithms for information processing and with the analysis and improvement of coding for information transfer. Shannon's paper was aimed at producing a general theory of communication about which he made the following preliminary observation:

> The fundamental problem of communication is that of reproducing at one point either exactly or approximately a message selected at another point. Frequently the messages have *meaning*; that is they refer to or are correlated according to some system with certain physical or conceptual entities. These semantic aspects of communication are irrelevant to the engineering problem. The significant aspect is

that the actual message is one *selected from a set* of possible messages. The system must be designed to operate for each possible selection, not just the one which will actually be chosen since this is unknown at the time of design.

Shannon sought a technical language, modeled on the study of thermodynamics, for defining and measuring information and methods for maximizing the flow of information in a communication system and for minimizing the entropy of, or "noise" in, the system. Information theory subsequently became enormously influential in shaping how specialists thought about the relationship of communication to technology, contributing also the basis of digital binary units (or, 0101 "bits") and 1024 bit packets that have become the standard coding method of contemporary information technologies and economies. Yet, one can read in Shannon's preliminary comment how information theory unapologetically requires first declaring the semantic (or meaning-oriented) aspects of communication not just less relevant but *irrelevant* to its enterprise. What is relevant to information theory is simply the *formal reproduction* of a message, exactly, across space and time.

This is to say that most of what human communication involves (tone, gesture, nuance, innuendo, intended meaning, unintended associations, negotiated meanings, social relations, etc.) is also irrelevant to information theory's formalist model of "information." "Information" is defined as a set of possible communications within a communicative system that is ideally binary in character (thus dividing knowledge clearly into relevant and irrelevant aspects). For the purposes of refining industrial telegraphy and telephony this made a great deal of sense (Shannon was working for Bell Labs at the time)—information theory suggested ways in which large quantities of data could be moved around with minimal errors. Its model of communication also offered a significant step in the direction of Bush's project of "mechanizing" knowledge through electronic means. The data archiving and processing industries that make us both optimistic and anxious today were born in this postwar environment and developed in tandem with computer engineering, guided by a social vision of integrated data management that was also shared by powerful institutional interests, especially by the U.S. Department of Defense for military and security purposes and by the National Science Foundation, for the improvement of national scientific datasharing. True to its modular, plurinodal character, this network eventually spilled outside of national ambitions and became international, developing new labels like "the world wide web" and "the internet." Theory and technology of "information" have subsequently allowed for the mass movement of mostly error-free data at amazing rates and scales (without them there would surely be none of the digital wonders of our age). Capitalizing upon such impressive technical achievements, It is perhaps little wonder that formalist understandings of ICTs are both possible and popular.

And yet this is not an either/or story. As noted at the outset, the immediation of the medial aspects of ICTs in the name of technology has by no means eclipsed medial talk and thinking about the internet. It also has not restricted poetic understandings, either allied with the technical use of ICTs (e.g., the ebullient technolibertarianism of *Wired* magazine) or in denial of such usage (e.g., those who actively pursue lifestyles that reject computers and other information technologies as irrelevant or dehumanizing). If anything, poetic, medial and formal understandings most often accompany each other, even becoming compressed in debates over media and their cultural impact. Case in point: television.

Mediated communities

The equation of media and culture is so banal that it doesn't appear to warrant much further commentary. It is hardly unusual to hear talk of the cultural influence of media or of media as cultural instruments, especially in "the media." In just the past week, I've read op-ed pieces on how televised violence and a "media culture of violence" inures children to violent behavior (as well as scholarly studies that both confirm and refute this link), I've read about the tendency of multichannel cable and the internet to foster (or simply reflect) cultural fragmentation, I've read commentaries in the alternative press on how corporate media are eroding the values and ideals of democratic society by fostering consumer culture and by naturalizing oligopolistic markets, and I've listened to a pledge drive on public radio make its case for supporting alternative viewpoints and its vital contribution to a "culture of informed debate." All point toward the same revolving certainty: media make culture but media, in turn, are cultural means, vehicles of cultural expression.

Talk about television has always been fabulously circuitous in this way, restlessly moving between appreciation for its medial power and for its immediated technological and instrumental features. TV proved the perfect muse for the medial philosophy of McLuhan just as it did for the dialectical poetic and formal attentions of Marxist media critic, Raymond Williams. In our society, I would say that medial and formal understandings of TV have generally been accentuated. But we should understand by now that this says less about the actual intrinsic features of the technical artifact or about its special mode of social mediation then it signals how people like us routinely encounter and engage televisual mediation.

Television sets are routine devices in our society, to be sure, and we routinely operate them in unremarkable ways. But their communicative channels are essentially one-way and so our engagement of television is experientially narrow, not as passive perhaps as the "mass pacification device" bumper stickers warn, but more passive than our use of telephones and many other ICTs nonetheless; we turn TV sets on, we surf channels, we watch content that has been prepared elsewhere. Even recent innovations in television like the proliferation of cable channels, TiVo, and on-demand services, all of which market themselves as putting more power in the viewer's hands, really only guarantee access to a larger volume of content and to more sophisticated filtering services. They don't actually allow us to make programming and budgetary decisions, to greenlight more comedies that we find funny or more dramas that we find compelling or more news programs that cover the issues we care about in the way we would like them to. The voting procedure on *American Idol* doesn't allow us to vote *American Idol* off the air. More to the point, a helpful instrument like TiVo does not authorize us to shift the market orientation of mass communication, which guarantees that commercial interests will remain central to both the revenue structure and programming orientation of mainstream television into the foreseeable future. As media historian Robert McChesney notes, the commercial orientation of mainstream broadcasting in the United States has never been put to a referendum, nor has it, until recently, even been made the subject of much political debate. All such decisions are made far away from our television sets, in highly restricted centers of televisual production, finance, and policy by people who may have us in mind, but who know rather little about us beyond our demographic identities and the metrics (e.g., Nielsen ratings) of our willingness to watch something they have broadcast. And, in fairness, we know even less about television decisionmakers and about the exigencies of their work, even if you happen to be an avid reader of *Variety*.

This is not a critical comment on television per se—the point could be extended to radio, to film, to novels, to *mass communication* more generally. Even in what has been termed the era of "consumer choice" and "reality programming" in broadcasting, very few of us experience the production of "culture" (meaning, mass or popular culture) poetically. We simply have no meaningful, experiential place in this apparatus, nor opportunities to do so, beyond marginal, and usually poorly funded, popular mass communication initiatives like lowpower radio, public access television, and vanity publishing. The paucity of experience varies from medium to medium, of course, and the video camera, for example, has become a considerably more routine companion over the past decade. But how often do we find our home videos circulated beyond our immediate circles of acquaintance? Even posting them on YouTube or a blog does not guarantee a broad audience. For the most part, when it comes to mass communication production, the institutional and professional hurdles to public participation are enormous, leaving us in the position of receivers or "consumers" of content prepared on our behalf. Thus, our sense of agency of what directs this media experience shifts from us to the technology or to "the media" itself.

It's important to realize that this rather estranged relationship to televisual media is not universal. Indeed, it is really a statement on the degree to which access to mass media production has been centralized and restricted within a society like our own. Under less restrictive circumstances, televisual media can be experienced very differently. Think, for example, of the Kayapo of Amazonia.

The Kayapo are a largely non-literate and fiercely independent society of several thousand Ge-speaking people living within Central Brazil who first came into sustained contact with Western culture in the 1950s when gold was discovered on their lands. While skirmishing with Brazilian miners and loggers, Kayapo recognized their need to formalize their claim to sovereignty over their lands in terms that the Brazilian government would recognize and respect. Some Kayapo became aware of video-making in the 1980s through contact with white Brazilian and international documentary filmmakers who traveled to their communities to document their changing way of life. Otherwise, they had very little experiential contact with mass communication: television and radio, for example, were only available at outposts on the edge of Kayapo territory. But a group of young Kayapo leaders immediately saw video's relevance to the intensifying political struggle with the Brazilian government to demarcate a sovereign Kayapo homeland. The anthropologist Terence Turner, with the help of the Spencer Foundation, arranged for video cameras and editing equipment to be made available to several Kayapo communities in the early 1990s. Kayapo immediately began documenting their protests with the government on video. They also made sure that Brazilian and international TV crews filmed them filming in order to demonstrate to the outside world their mastery of Western technology and to raise awareness of their political cause outside of Brazil. To this end, they even filmed and edited their own documentary videos on Kayapo culture for non-Kayapo consumption. And, their strategy worked. Eventually with the help of international human rights organizations like The Rainforest Foundation, and the publicity generated by their videos, the Kayapo were able to win their reserve from Brasilia.

Meanwhile, in the United States, some anthropologists criticized Turner's participation in this project, arguing that it was not empowering for Kayapo to use Western "visual technologies" like video and photography since whatever political gains they enjoyed were being offset by the loss of their indigenous cultural techniques and traditions. Turner responded that these critics couldn't have been more wrong. Kayapo cultural traditions were not of "the culture of the ear and mouth" variety to begin with— long before their use of video, they had developed sophisticated visual and aesthetic practices of their own. More to the point, Kayapo did not themselves see video as a threat to their traditional way of life nor did they view their cultural traditions as fragile enough to be endangered through contact with Western technology. What they saw in video was precisely a messaging instrument, one that they could use to combat the genuine threats to their cultural autonomy they recognized in the Brazilian government and Brazilian economic interests. Indeed, Kayapo became avid and canny videomakers for the better part of a decade, not only documenting political events, but taping cultural performances and, at least in one case, producing a fictional video dramatization of what would happen to miners who were caught illegally entering their land (in a word, nothing good). Then, without much fanfare, their political purpose achieved and their video equipment deteriorated by the tropical environment, Kayapo largely gave up videomaking by the late 1990s.

What is most striking about what has since come to be known as the Kayapo Video Project is how matter-of-factly Kayapo picked up and later dropped video technology. This particularly unsettled the skeptics who found it difficult to believe that Kayapo could really treat video cameras in such an off-handed way—they looked restlessly for evidence that cameras were technologically transforming Kayapo culture as well, subtly dominating them and forcing them to westernize culturally. The skeptics' certainty of the pernicious medial and formal qualities of the medium wonderfully epitomizes the divergent social experiences and expectations of televisual media at play. Kayapo did not primarily experience video cameras as technical or medial powers; they had no doubts about their power to control video poetically, in large part because they actually had the cameras in their hands and were actively integrating them into familiar political and aesthetic practices for specific social purposes. The skeptics meanwhile were living in a different social environment of media. People like them (and like us) do a lot more watching than making media, and this heightens our experience of them as transactional forces and technical forms beyond us, enveloping us, yet insulated from our own cultural powers. How many times have you watched a particularly crappy television program and said to yourself, "If *I* were a network executive..."? Well, you're not. Since the cameras really aren't in our hands, it's hard for us to believe that televisual media are simply instrumental. Beneath suspicion of the Kayapo Video Project lurked a certain envy of greater power over mass culture, I think, that quickly turned into a bitter generalization of the contemporary

Western experience of mass media to all peoples and all media, everywhere.

So, returning to more familiar territory, let's not count the poetic out altogether—this is the key to understanding why we are ultimately so certain of the equation between culture and media. A feeling of anxiety or estrangement from mass communication does not mean that it is impossible to understand the power of a medium like television poetically. But what happens is that the struggle for immediation typically moves to a different plane. Reduced experiential intimacy creates the opportunity to enhance fantasied intimacy. In keeping with the "mass-ness" of our experience of a medium like television, we shift our basis of poetic certainty from our more immediate lives and relations into more abstract schemes of "we-ness" and "they-ness." We tend to highlight collective senses of instrumentality, speaking of the agenda of "corporate culture" or of how "national culture" influences (and is reflected in) the character of television. Suddenly, "the nation" and "corporations" are glossed as holistic collectivities, collectivities that behave poetically, as though they were persons. Perhaps we don't approve of the cultural agendas we impart to corporate media or nationalism. But securing a clear agent that is accountable for why popular culture looks the way it does restores a sense of the poetic to popular culture that holds open the possibility that a different poetic force could eventually generate a popular culture we found more agreeable. Yet, this is a delicate compromise since a collective poetic or instrumental force is still at considerable remove from personal experience, "the nation" or "corporate culture" being, in the final analysis, no less abstract entities than "the media." One finds especially that talk of the relationship of media and culture tends to compress immedial and medial understandings in ways that are less familiar in discussions of media as messaging instruments and information technologies. The boundaries between the poetic, the medial and the formal become less distinct and the distribution of powers less clear. Culture becomes medial and media cultural.

I'd like to point out that this kind of conceptual fluidity is not owed to a lack of sophistication in popular talk about mass media like television. It is entirely common to specialized scholarly discourse on mass media as well. Popular phrases in media studies like "mediated culture" and "cultural mediation" often turn out to be truisms upon closer analysis. And, yet, they are also accepted as the state of the art in much media scholarship. Actually, I can't think of a better example of the compression of poetic, medial, and formal understandings I'm describing than probably the most influential academic study of culture and media written in the past twenty-five years, Benedict Anderson's *Imagined Communities*.

If you are unfamiliar with the book, Anderson's basic argument in *Imagined Communities* is that our ability to imagine ourselves as members of a modern national community, to feel, for example, that we share some common identity with 295 million odd other Americans, the vast majority of whom we will never meet, is owed to a fundamental shift in understanding of the world that was set into motion in Europe in the

15th and 16th centuries. Anderson argues that a sense of belonging to a nation required first a consciousness of living within a "sociological organism" moving through linear time. Individuals like us interchangeably enter and exit the organism, but the organism, the nation, is believed to live on regardless of the fate of its component members, with its own spirit, its own territory, and its own history. Anderson points out that this is a different understanding of social belonging and identity then that which prevailed, for example, in the estates system of medieval Europe, which was at once more localist and more universalist than the national-sociological organism and which would never have recognized the members of different estates as being interchangeable with one another.

Anderson then charts a historical convergence of three forces that made it possible to "think the nation," an "explosive, interaction between a system of production and productive relations (capitalism), a technology of communications (print), and the fatality of human linguistic diversity."

Capitalism, in its way, restlessly searched to open new markets and the invention and proliferation of print technology in 15th and 16th century Europe created an enormous enterprise in books. Over time, Anderson argues, print enhanced the social importance of European vernacular languages (e.g., English, French, German, etc.) relative to the sacred religious language of Latin, because vernacular language publication attracted wider audiences and thus better economies of scale for commercial publishing. Mass vernacular publishing laid important cultural foundations for nationalism by cultivating certain linguistic dialects as national "standards," which were taken over by states as their languages of administration and which gradually displaced the linguistic diversity of spoken dialects, thus linguistically unifying European populations at roughly the scale of "the nation." At the same time, Anderson describes how the modern print genres of newspapers and novels offered crucial literary models for the sociological organism of the nation: the serial character of newspapers epitomized a sense of linear time and historical depth and novels provided imaginary worlds within which actors could be connected in space and time by intersecting narrative lines without being immediately known to one another. Since both newspapers and novels were widely read, at least among elites, they could thus provide cultural models for new understandings of social belonging and identity, new understandings that would eventually be utilized by 19th century nationalist political movements.

You can see right away how medial and formal attentions deeply influence Anderson's portrait. On the one hand, Anderson assumes that print technology has the intrinsic capacity to stimulate new senses of space and time. On the other hand, it is the medial power of capitalism, its drive to create larger spheres of transaction and circulation that propels both vernacular publishing and national imagination forward.

Yet the importance of poetic attentions emerges in a later chapter on "creole pioneers," where Anderson notes that nationalism only really began to take shape in the administrative and intellectual cultures of European colonies in the 17th and 18th centuries. Europe itself was still dominated by dynastic states and the social conservatism of the estates system. But, in the colonies, the estates system had a lesser hold. The distance from Europe meant that local elites retained considerable political authority and social autonomy. Culturally, they both identified with Europe and didn't. Most importantly, colonial elites, especially state functionaries and intellectuals, enjoyed considerable geographic and social mobility—through their travels, correspondences, and social networks they came to understand the colonial administrative units first as distinct, unified polities and later as national organisms socially and culturally separate from the European homeland. Anderson's key point is that creole pioneers like Benjamin Franklin in North America or Simon Bolivar in South America took it upon themselves to fashion the content of the organisms. Whether politically or culturally, creole pioneers worked to define particular national characters and identities modeled upon their own experience of creole (colonial) identity and sovereignty. The experience and agency of creole pioneers, especially the movements of national liberation that they helped to craft, became decisive for shaping a political-cultural form, modern nationalism, that then migrated back to Europe in the 19th century and was subsequently exported to the rest of the world through European imperialism.

The brilliance of Anderson's book is that it manages to somehow keep all three balls (poetic, medial and formal attentions) in the air without necessarily asserting the ultimate priority of one over the others. This also explains, in part, why the book is so widely read and referenced—in a sense, there's no need to look beyond it since it already contains within itself the entire media/culture debate. At the same time, *Imagined Communities* makes scholars remarkably restless. Many have interpreted Anderson's approach as a failure to commit one way or the other, as a kind of half-baked "splitting differences" in lieu of a real argument. I don't think that Anderson deliberately intended to split the difference between poetic, medial and formal concerns but *Imagined Communities* does so elegantly, so much so that each faction seems to read a different book. But, owing to the unmistakable residue of other attentions in the book, no faction seems entirely satisfied with it.

What the uneven scholarly reception of an approach like Anderson's teaches us is that debates over media and culture tend to specialize within the poetic/medial/formal triad, producing factions whose arguments are drawn into the orbit of one or another certainty: that media are ultimately messaging instruments, tools of human intentions and relations, or that media are ultimately technologies of communication and information, with intrinsic technical features and powers of their own, or that media are conduits of cultural and social mediation, beholden ultimately only to their own transactional logics, like Marx's capital or McLuhan's medium-as-message. Each argument appears to preclude the validity of the others. And, yet, this is only because of the specialization and polarization of attentions in the first place. They only seem contradictory if one accepts them on their own mutually exclusionary terms. What I argue in the conclusion of this essay is that these certainties are complementary rather than contradictory and therefore a *multiattentional* approach is actually the best method of understanding media we have available to us.

A digression on media excess

But, before getting to that conclusion, please allow me one final digression. This essay has been working all along with a specific conclusion in mind. Yet it feels a bit too tidy, too contained, to me. We have to bear in mind the elephant in the corner that there is nothing at all tidy and contained about media. If there was, we wouldn't feel so compelled to understand them. So, to correct for this essay's own tempering, immediating character, I would like to return briefly to the sense of overwhelming mediation with which I began the essay.

I have taught undergraduate courses on media for ten years now. And, I always begin by asking students to take stock of what they know about media. Most recently, only a few days ago, in fact, I asked a class to discuss whether they thought media had power over us. In large part because of the very framing of the question, the responses split along roughly poetic and medial lines, with some students emphasizing individual power over media and others emphasizing the powers of capitalism and media over us. The medialists pointed to the commercial, corporate character of mass media and argued that no matter what one watched, one was getting the same market-oriented programming saturated with advertising and consumer messages. The poeticists countered that despite the limitations of mass media, abundant alternative media existed, with different messages and orientations. Ultimately, they argued, corporate media or not, we have the power to define how we engage media—after all, the remotes are in our hands. The medialists shook their heads and said that whatever power we did have had the decks of mass media and capitalism already stacked against it—in the end, we didn't have real autonomy so much as a kind of weak "consumer choice" among limited options. The debate went back and forth for several minutes until a hitherto silent student, obviously a little exasperated with the exchange, commented, "The thing is, media are just there, everywhere. You can't get away from them."

His remark was an excellent reminder that beneath the fineries of debate over the location and proportion of powers in media we find again the experiential fact of media excess, that "media are just *there, everywhere*." This contemporary fact of excess is, to my mind, the root of our sense that our lives are mediated more so now than ever before and the occasion for various projects of immediation.

Excess is that aspect of the experience of mediation that spills outside of our usual strategies of media talk and media thinking. It is therefore a phenomenon that is difficult to write about. Excess is euphoric, unsettling, nauseating. It is the encounter with media messages cascading everywhere, engaging us from so many different directions with unpredictable timing, producing so many minor ripples and eddies of effect. Hot news stories often have this excessive quality to them, as though they originate from nowhere and then, once they are circulating, that there is nowhere to hide from them. Here's one you may have heard of: Mel Gibson, speeding, driving drunk, is pulled over and issued a DUI. It gets into the national news feeds almost immediately after he is booked at the local police station (in Malibu, there are journalists whose job it is basically to wait for these kinds of things to happen). A few hours later several pages of the original police report are posted on a celebrity news website. And, suddenly, a good news-story (from a celebrity news point of view) becomes a must-read one; the report details how Gibson resisted arrest and let loose a rant laced with anti-Semitic and sexist remarks.

By the morning the original story line (DUI bust) and the new story line (Gibson's anti-Semitic rant) are off and running. Later that morning, Google news lists over four hundred independent hits as news organizations across the world have picked up and re-publicized the story. If you hadn't been paying attention to the early hours of the story, and if you didn't know how news organizations continuously monitor their competitors' news output and re-allocate resources to take advantage of high-profile "breaking news" like this, then you might believe what happens over the next 72 hours is the work of some kind of full-blown perpetuum news mobile. New substory lines branch off and proliferate at a fabulous rate as Gibson apologizes first for his alcoholism and "despicable remarks," then after the anti-Semitic rant is confirmed,

for his prejudice as well. Leaders of the Jewish community make public statements. Celebrity image managers
weigh in. Network executives weigh in. The op/ed
commentary begins to pour in: ranging from sympathy
for a deluded, hounded man to calculations of
Gibson's loss of public good will to "I knew he was an
Anti-Semite ever since *The Passion of the Christ*."
Gibson's police mugshot is everywhere, including the
cover of *USA Today*, the best-selling national daily.
Updates on the story (even when there is little new
"news" to behold) are being pushed everywhere, in
newspapers, on radio, both public and private, in the
internet, on morning and late-night TV shows.
Meanwhile, even the most media-impoverished of us
would realize that something is going on. I overhear
people mentioning or laughing about the story in
coffee shops, a local deli, a gym, and in a pool hall.
Ironic commentary arrives in my email inbox from
colleagues across three continents. Boom, boom,
boom, as McLuhan would have said. If I were to feign
ignorance and to ask what was going on, I would no
doubt lose some social face—how could I be so "out of
touch?" Later in the day, Google news offers over
1,500 links on the main story-line, which now resem-
bles a budding potato: "Gibson's tirade causes
Hollywood Uproar," "Gibson faces time in jail,"
"Gibson invited to Jewish museum," and "Mad Mel's
passion needs to be curbed" (among hundreds of
others…).

In a few more hours, the story will slowly
diminish within news cycles, displaced by other breaking news, and eventually it will disappear altogether. By

the time this essay is published, it will be a faded memory. But, for the moment, it is there, everywhere. Its echo effect is impressive. The main story becomes the inspiration for countless further acts of analysis and representation, for commentary on Anti-Semitism, on redemption, on our obsession with celebrity news, and so on and on. Not to mention, of course, the excuse for a little irony and laughter between friends and strangers.

One Mel Gibson news story hardly seems substantial enough to legitimate a medial understanding of the power of "the media." It's too easily rationalized, domesticated, made light of (in just the way I have done). Nor is it insubstantial enough to reward belief in media as a tool subject to our choices and wills (after all, it seems there's nowhere to turn at this moment where one can escape the message).

It may interest you to know that news journalists themselves—the artisans of excess in this case—might be similarly torn in how they viewed the story, but for different reasons. Given their intimate familiarity with media-making, journalists are more apt to think of the dynamics of media-making poetically and formally, reproducing their self-image as canny professionals working to beat "the system" and to fulfill their vocation to inform the public. "The system" here could equivalently refer to Hollywood insiderism or to corporate news. In either case, journalists see a formal apparatus of censorial power as their natural enemy. The news journalists with whom I have worked largely belong to the latter camp, those who disdain the recent trend toward more celebrity reporting in mainstream

news. They view celebrity news' heightened importance as a sign of the invasive market managerialism
afflicting media organizations today and are very
concerned about what this trend may signal about the
future practice of news journalism. You see, news journalists have medial anxieties as well, just different ones.
They are concerned with what they view as the breakdown of barriers between the commercial and professional domains of news journalism within media organizations and how this breakdown has made stories of
the Gibson variety a new priority in mainstream news.
But they aren't anxious about media excess per se; they
are much more likely to say that their strategies for
containing and managing the abundance of media
messages they face on a daily basis are successful.
Personally, I'm not sure that they actually are more
successful than the rest of ours but I think that the fact
that journalists are privileged media-makers allows
them to witness the tangible results of their work mediated all the time. Not unlike the Kayapo, they thus
have a more intimate and secure understanding of how
their media messages are produced and circulated.
And, that's an incomparable advantage for a poetic
understanding of media, especially mass media.

In any event, the Gibson story is just the
narrowest snapshot of media excess. A complete
portrait would be endless and impossible to narrate
effectively. It would have to take into account the multiple modes of mediation that cut across our lives on a
daily basis. For me, this would not only include the
range of news media just profiled, but oral dialogue,
music, books, film, advertising, telephony and cellular

telephony, wireless services, email and the internet. Among these are a subset of media engagements that I directly and voluntarily initiate in a goal-oriented sort of way and many others that seem to find me whether I want them to or not. Excess is epitomized by the surreal echoes of mass mediated stories and cultural forms across the landscape of everyday life. Like this strange experience I keep having that wherever I go in little Ithaca, New York—a place far removed from American public cultural production centers like Los Angeles and Manhattan—I hear young white men yelling things like "Wassup!" and "I'm Rick James, bitch!" at each other. If I stop a moment and try to connect the dots, I can trace a cause-effect chain back through popular film and television comedy to Martin Lawrence and Dave Chappelle and think about why it would be appealing and liberating for young white men to borrow their phrases. And, yet, who has the luxury of time to stop and to think about where all these media messages are coming from and where they are headed? Excess can be mesmerizing, thrilling in short bursts, but also exhausting. So, like news journalists, we all have containment strategies—ways of rationalizing, filtering, and ignoring media—for reducing the excessive qualities of mass communication. However, successful insulation requires active suppression of excess. Therefore, insulation must be maintained—and, this requires energy and invites unresolved tension. Mostly, the effort to manage media excess leaves us feeling a bit like we're trying to manage an umbrella during a windy downpour.

Moreover, we all face situations when insulation becomes virtually impossible. This state is captured in another recent neologism: "media over-load." Have you taken a walk through Times Square recently? Try it at rush hour. Pure excess. It's an extreme example to be sure, but in addition to the social mediation of the city (the pressing crowds, the noise, the cars) one is confronted with every imaginable medium of mass communication as well (from music to billboards to street theater to the internet to film to television), all blinking, flashing, swirling around, seeking to attract and hold your attention for a messaging moment. For most people not inured to this scene through routine exposure, even a few minutes in Times Square are enough to inspire feelings of both awe and dread, of teetering on the brink of an unknowable medial abyss. Of course, even Times Square is neither intrinsically nor absolutely medial. For example, I could do a great deal of research and write probably a very long book that patiently analyzed and explained the poetic and formal agencies embedded within every single message one encounters in Times Square, from the science and engineering of the billboards and digital screens to the planning of urban renewal and tourism in Manhattan to the creative work of the advertising and publicity campaigns represented there to the politics of corporate sponsoring. It might be a life's work but such a book would, in the end, be informative and containing. Sitting at home in quiet comfort, reading it might even have some therapeutic value. But there would also be something hopeless about such a venture, like the Middlemarchian "key to all mythologies." Because a scholarly text, no matter how extensive and well-documented, wouldn't capture at all the parallel experience, the thrills and anxiety, of entering such an intense nexus of social mediation.

So what do we do about media excess and media overload? I've already suggested that the experience of mass media and social mediation contributes richly to our impression that media are "the message" of our lives and to the increasingly common wisdom that our powers to think and to act are contingent upon media technologies and mass communication like never before. Some of us, like McLuhan, even seem to find solace in our apparent subjection to "the media" as though nothing could be more natural. And, yet, hidden away in that solace is a wonderful poetic twist. Media researchers have long noted what they describe as a "third person effect" in talk about the power of media. In other words, people are quite certain as to the medial and formal powers of media, but people also typically think this power is stronger over other people than over them. Moreover, this sense is inversely proportional to how well they know someone else. In other words, the more distant the contact you have to someone the greater your certainty that that person is influenced by media, often negatively. Similarly, opinion polls consistently demonstrate a strong popular belief that media representations of sexuality and violence influence youth behavior (the third person effect holds true here as well, by the way, since it is most often adults who are called upon to comment on children's perceptions and behavior). But in the vast archive of media scholarship that has been devoted to this topic over the past forty years, there are absolutely no consistent findings as to whether the suspected media power over social behavior can be scientifically validated. Each study refutes the previous one. The problem with "social science" in this respect is that there are no independent variables in social experience, no aspects of human social relations that are not influenced by all the others. Thus, experimental methods derived from laboratory science and applied to social issues typically yield inconclusive results. In this case, given what we know of the many pathways of media excess, how can one really measure media exposure to an acceptable degree of certainty? How can one determine precisely how the media messages children (the usual class of victims) receive through television (the usual culprit) interact with the other kinds of messages people encounter from a variety of sources near and far (friends, parents, teachers, non-televisual media, for example), not to mention determine whether specific actions were motivated by these received messages?

And, yet, the absence (or partiality) of scientific corroboration will do nothing to weaken popular wisdom in the formative power of media over us (or, maybe more accurately, over other people). What we need to realize is that this is because all this talk about television, violence and sexuality really has very little to do with television, violence and sexuality. What we are sensing and saying is that there is a great density of social mediation wreathing us, including, increasingly, informational powers and messages, over which we have no poetic, let alone instrumental, control. We are concerned with how these forces may be affecting and afflicting us, but, since we have at the same time experiential knowledge of our own poetic, instrumental powers, we're even more concerned about how these forces are affecting and afflicting our more vulnerable neighbors, especially our children.

In the end, we come full circle back to where we began, with the fact of excess and the feeling that our lives are saturated with, and defined by, media. I think it would be crazy not to acknowledge this feeling's validity—social truths like "our lives are mediated," after all, don't appear at random, but rather for the good reason that their attentions tend to confirm common experiences of the world, in this case, experiences of the transactional and translocational dimensions of mass communication and social mediation.

Yet, as in the case of "the media," social truths also gloss and formalize experience, they take the fluidity and contingency of experiential knowledge and give it solid, objective, even ontological frames. In our case, we find the experience of mediation becoming the truth of "being mediated." Why distinguish between them? Because the social truth in question formalizes some experiential attentions and not others. One gets the impression that (1) because of the expanded sphere of social mediation and (2) because of the heightened attention it subsequently received (culminating in "medial philosophy" among other things) that, ergo, mediation is, in fact, the defining condition of our life. But this logic is faulty because it ignores that the attention we commit to managing excessive mediation prompts us to pay considerably less heed to parallel, but less spectacular, experiences of being unmediated, what I described in the first section of the essay as the stubborn plurality of human immediacies.

It reminds me of the way that we also hear so much about the complexity of the modern world but less about its comparative simplicities. And, simplicity is enormously appealing in many ways—those politicians and religious figures who specialize in simplicity have done well for themselves in recent years, perhaps as a direct response to the expert's mantra that everything is always more complex than we think it is. To the expert we could say: Yes, it can be more complex but it can also be more straightforward. That is a question primarily of how we direct and scale our attentions. One can find limitless complexity in any object of attention but one can also find simple forms and relations and the one approach is not intrinsically more truthful than the other. Or, more precisely, they engage different levels of truth. In our case, if we pay sufficient attention to the immediacies and intimacies that also characterize our lives, then the social truth that "our lives are mediated" suddenly rings a little hollow.

Yet, since we've managed to be so blunt about philosophy up to this point, though, I feel compelled to note that appealing to immediacy is also an old trick in the philosopher's bag. From Plato to Nietzsche to Heidegger, there is a tendency to disparage pernicious philosophical obsessions with metaphysics, speculation, and mediation through a call for renewed attention to the problem of being. It's a good move since philosophy, as an expert practice, does typically branch out into speculative, metaphysical and technical concerns. Even if the specialist's "return to being" can often end up no less esoteric and experientially distant than the bad old metaphysics.

But I'm not arguing that media and mediation are matters of appearance as immedia and immediation are matters of being. Mediation is real, as real as anything in human experience. With apologies to Rousseau, there is no natural state of man beyond society and history. Where there is exchange, motion, and language there is mediation. And, just because mediation typically challenges our ability to know more extensive social relations with intimate certainty does not make those relations any less real. It's like Freud's model of the unconscious—not all psychic activity may be available to our consciousness but that doesn't make these deep psychic domains any less consequential for how we think and act.

What I am trying to say, if I were to put this in a more philosophical language, is that mediation and immediation are dually aspects of being. There is obviously no way to understand humanity, at once social, historical, biotic, dynamic, ordered, aware, unconscious, imaginative, reflective, habitual, without some sense of both. But our experiential knowledge tends to polarize between them. This has always been the case but the specialization of attentions and knowledge in contemporary society has developed huge encampments of experts on all sides whose arguments have become increasingly exclusionary and oppositional. Today, we hear medial prophets, latter day McLuhans, continue to startle us with the idea that media are the message of human experience. And, we will hear poets and technicians of media remind us of the ubiquity and efficacy of media even as they reassure us that media are really ultimately nothing more than instruments, technologies, or means of cultural expression. Therefore, the basic challenge of understanding media today is how not to be lured into thinking about media just one way or another.

Understanding media (a multiattentional approach)

So how *should* we understand media? I mentioned above that certainty is an inevitable aspect of human knowledge. Even critical knowledge, pragmatic knowledge, relativist knowledge, full-blown anything-goes antifoundationalist postmodern knowledge; all these specialized ways of knowing take certainties for granted and propose their own, however *contingently*. So, the real question is not how to dismantle our habits of understanding media—we have, after all, our certainties for good reasons—but how also to cultivate new habits of understanding media that allow us to appreciate the contributions of those different certainties simultaneously without allowing some to dominate, dispel or trivialize the others.

To those who have specialized in poetic, medial and formal attentions concerning media, to those who gone a little farther and developed theories based upon those specialized attentions, to those who have specialized enough in those theories to have become partisans of one position of another, to all of them I would say that the hardest thing is to accept is that all three ways of understanding media are equivalently correct. To be precise, none is absolutely correct and they are not "the same" but given their complementarity of attentions, each is as correct as the other. I believe that careful attention to any medium (taking both mediation and immediation into consideration) can only result in that conclusion. So, do we stop there, splitting the difference as it were? Well, balancing poetic, medial, and formal attentions as Anderson does is a good start and a way of engaging the world that should encourage more thinking and talking about the living history of media around us.

But, to return to the conflict of attentions described above, what we really need is a *multiattentional* approach to understanding media, one that seeks to hold medial, poetic and formal, intimate and abstract, rational, anxious and fantastic understandings of media in focus at the same time. What we need is the ability to maintain multiple attentional foci simultaneously in media talk and thinking. Only this would allow us to dissolve the conceptual impasses in everyday and expert talk and thinking about media. This sounds like a scholar's concern, I'm sure, but the point is very simple: why look at things just one way? After all, attention belongs to all of us, and developing and differentiating attentions is part of all of our life projects. In addition, all of us would profit from trying to understand media beyond the limits of poeticist, medialist and formalist partisanship. My caution is that holding multiple attentions in focus is a method much easier advocated than accomplished. There's a reason why we commonly understand media in the simplified terms that we do. Because it helps us to establish certainty more quickly, efficiently, and decisively, regardless of the orientation of the certainty in question. My contribution here, I hope, has been to make specialized singular attentions a little less certain. But I don't imagine that multiattentionality is an easy trick to master; an appropriate comparison would probably be something like teaching your vocal chords to make two independent sounds at the same time. With practice and guidance, it can and has been done, but it doesn't lend itself to familiar melodies. Multiattentional engagements won't, at least at first, provide narratives that seem to have clear story lines but will likely seem more like this essay, ping-ponging between attentions while trying not to get caught lingering too long on any one of them.

Nevertheless, outlining a multiattentional mode of understanding media has been my goal in this essay. It is, if you like, my "paradigm," prickles and all. But, I realize that a text like this one is a very limited medium. For it to become an intervention capable of changing habits, it would have to participate in a social project, just as medial philosophy and the immediation of communication technology are social projects. So, as much as it is anything else, a guidebook for instance, this essay is an invitation to others frustrated with the routines of contemporary media talk and thinking, an invitation to concern yourself anew with understanding media. ■

Also available from Prickly Paradigm Press:

continued